A Sacred Foundation

Michael Farris
and
L. Reed Elam

Loyal Publishing
www.loyalpublishing.com

CONTENTS

INTRODUCTION

Marriages at Risk

*A*s typical Christian home schoolers we seem to have all the ingredients for perfect families: two parents in the home, strong commitment to the family as the key unit in society, convictions that won't quit in the face of persecution, beliefs that if God says it, we'll do it—period. It would certainly appear that we have all it takes for great marriages and happy families.

So why do we hear about so many divorces among committed Christian home school couples?

At Home School Legal Defense Association (HSLDA), we hear of new divorces—usually the result of adultery and abandonment—on a regular basis. Perhaps home schoolers are not divorcing as frequently as couples in society at large, but far too often nonetheless. And it's not just the rank and file home schoolers who are leaving their spouses. Even some leaders of the home school movement are breaking their marriage vows.

Adultery, divorce, and remarriage have invaded the ranks of leadership—striking more than one leader's family. One state home school leader met his "new woman" via a computer chat service. He later divorced his wife to continue the relationship. And despite the fact that he had previously testified in favor of home schooling in the state legislature, he testified against it in his own family's custody trial. He wanted to avoid some of his financial responsibilities to his family by forcing his wife out of the home and into the workplace.

What Is Going On?

Why are some home schoolers' marriages falling apart? Marital unfaithfulness is on the rise, even among Christian couples. Just like the rest of society we are paying a price for living in post-Christian twenty-first century America. Sexual temptations bombard us at every turn. For many the temptation is too great; they give in.

Three Contributing Factors

We believe marital stability is adversely affected by three influences:

Adverse Influence #1

Most Christian home schoolers desire academic success for their children. They work hard to give their children challenging material and work with reasonable diligence to guide their children toward academic excellence. But, academics is not the main reason Christian families home school.

Vickie and I (Mike) began home schooling in 1982 with the expectation that we would simply "break even" on the academic side of things. Our real desire was to develop Christlike character in our oldest daughter, Christy.

Even though Christy attended a Christian school in kindergarten and first grade, she was already beginning to develop the classic pattern of peer-dependency. After only two years of attending a good Christian school, she cared more for the opinions of her six-year-old friends than she did for the opinions of her parents. Since "foolishness is bound up in the heart of a child" (Proverbs 22:15a), we felt that the only method available for us to rescue her from developing her opinions from other little "fools" was to have her spend more time with her parents than she did with her friends.

We have never tried to shield any of our children from exposure to other children (although we have avoided particular individuals from time to time). They have a range of friends and acquaintances from both Christian and non-Christian circles. The home schooling environment, however, allows our children to model their parents' behavior and attitudes rather than their friends' behavior and attitudes. We believe this is the best method for developing Christian character in our children.

Our family is not alone in saying that home schooling has been truly successful in accomplishing our top goal of Christian character development. Children who have been raised in home schooling, including ours, are not perfect, nor are they universally of high Christian character. But the overwhelming majority of home-schooled Christian children are far more spiritually mature than their parents were at similar ages.

This was true in my case even though I was saved at a young age, raised in a Christian home, and attended a solid Bible teaching church from my earliest years. The Christian teaching I learned at church and home were consistently neutralized as I spent hours and hours in a school system that was under a national court order to exclude God from the curriculum. When a child is trained in godliness at home, school, and church, it makes sense that the child will be more likely to experience positive spiritual development than the child who is in an educational system where people start having legal heart attacks if anyone ever mentions God in a favorable manner.

The most important command Jesus gave His disciples is found in the Great Commission: "Therefore go and make disciples of all the nations, baptizing them in the name of the Father and of the Son and of the Holy Spirit, and teaching them to obey everything I have commanded you. And surely I am with you always, to the very end of the age" (Matthew 28:19-20). The church has misinterpreted Jesus' command. He did not tell us to make disciples *in* all nations. He called us to make disciples *of* all nations.

How do you disciple a nation? As usual, God gives us an example in Scripture. Through Jacob's descendents, God desired to disciple a nation (Genesis 35). God expected Jacob to disciple his twelve sons—for his sons would become the patriarchs of the twelve tribes of Israel. They, in turn, were expected to disciple their sons and daughters, and so on. Discipled families were to become discipled clans. Discipled clans were to become discipled tribes. And ultimately, discipled tribes were supposed to become a discipled nation. God's plan from the beginning hinged on effective discipleship within families.

The family, rather than the church or government, is God's first choice of human institutions in which discipleship is to occur. God never intended the government to be the agency of discipleship, and the role of the church in discipleship is really a catch-up program for people who were not discipled by their own parents.

Discipleship differs from other forms of teaching in that discipleship cares more about a person's actions and attitudes than his level of knowledge. The most effective way to disciple someone (as well as to monitor his progress) is to live with him day in and day out.

The very best discipleship method is modeling. Psychologists explain modeling as a way for children to learn by watching and interacting with others of their species. When parents invest large amounts of time with their children, they are training them in godliness as they sit down, as they walk along the way, and as they go through the normal actions of life (Deuteronomy 6:7-9). This is what God had in mind when He designed the family.

Moment by moment instruction was much more frequent when children did not attend institutional schools for academic instruction. Parents worked alongside their children in the fields, in the carpenter's shop, in the kitchen, or wherever they worked throughout the day, enabling parents to devote constant hours of conversation with their children. Parents were able to transfer their values in a natural manner.

Not all parents transferred good values, as the biblical story of Lot clearly illustrates (Genesis 19). Nevertheless, the ability to transmit values, whether positive or negative, is largely a factor of how much time parents spend with their children.

Modern life requires children to devote a great deal of time to academic instruction. Home schooling allows parents and children to have sufficient time together to achieve simultaneous success in the modern field of academics and the historical role of "values-transmission" or what we call discipleship.

Home schooling is creating thousands of little disciples who have the real potential of launching a white-hot movement of God. We believe the Christian home schooling movement is sparking a revival that is unequaled anywhere else in our society. (A revival is a phenomenon when one generation gets "set on fire for God" and shakes up a nation.)

Our children are the generation that is being set on fire for God. Home schoolers are developing both academic and spiritual success of such an unusual degree that will indeed shake up our nation (if we can just hold on to a measure of freedom for a few more years). Most

revivals eventually become lukewarm as the next generation's commitment to the values of the movement
wanes, but we believe this revival has the capability of
becoming permanent. When our children follow our
example of discipleship by becoming home schooling
parents, we are much more likely to ensure that generation after generation will be even more spiritual than the
generation that preceded them.

What do the potential for revival and incidence of
divorce among home school families have in common?
Spiritual warfare. If we understand the opportunity for
spiritual success that is inherent in home schooling, we
can be guaranteed that Satan understands this as well.
He wants to defeat any force that has the potential of
launching a permanent spiritual revival.

One of Satan's most obvious strategies is to attack
our marriages. Satan cannot destroy anyone's marriage
on his own, but he can work with our own propensity to
sin and supply us with plenty of discouragement and
temptation to make sure that the situation is right if we
should choose to sin.

Recently I talked with a home schooling mom whom
I had worked with a few months earlier concerning an
HSLDA legal problem. She and her husband adhered to
the "black belt" approach to home schooling with their
seven children. They seemed committed to every
advanced concept that is popular in the home schooling
movement. To my great dismay, the mom told me her
husband had demonstrated a lack of one very important
commitment—a commitment to marital fidelity.

Shortly after the HSLDA legal situation was over, the husband began an adulterous affair with a woman from work. The wife was so devastated that she rejected not only her husband's superficial "repentance," but she also rejected God. She rebuffed me when I mentioned God in our conversation. She said, "I don't want to hear anymore of that God talk."

Satan won that battle. Seven young lives that had every potential for spiritual vitality were permanently handicapped because their Dad decided that his momentary sexual happiness was more important than his wife and children's spiritual well-being. How does a caring, Christian father arrive at this point? No loving, rational father would think such a thing unless he began to believe the satanic lie that he could sin without consequences.

I believe that home schoolers are going to face an unusual degree of satanic temptation and attacks simply because we have unusually high prospects for spiritual success with our children. And those prospects have multiplied potential for long-range impact on generations to come. The enemy of our soul is going to take every opportunity to break up our marriages because of the dynamic spiritual potential our families represent.

Adverse Influence #2

A significant yet unrecognized factor that promotes divorce is dating. Dating forms habits of heart and mind that steer people toward marital dissatisfaction, infidelity, and ultimately divorce. The "wonderful world of dating" creates the atmosphere and expectations of boy-girl relationships far earlier than is appropriate.

If a young person "falls in love" at thirteen or fourteen years of age, emotional commitments are made and inevitably broken. Pieces of one's heart are given away. After a while, emotional entanglements lead to physical activities. Handholding and kissing are exciting at first, but as dating relationships become more intimate, the desire for greater physical intimacy increases between couples. After one has been a part of the dating scene for three, four, or five years, the natural physical response to romantic love is sexual intercourse.

The "condom lobby" argues that all kids are having sex—it's unavoidable. The answer—if you can't stop them, help them by making condoms readily available.

Most Christian conservatives argue that unmarried teens can abstain from sex. Conservatives assert that we should set high standards for physical purity (which is usually defined as no sexual intercourse before marriage), and we should expect our children to live up to this standard.

Don't misunderstand. We all need to expect this standard of purity (and a whole lot higher standard as well). But there is a certain element of truth in Jocelyn Elder's cynical and evil arguments. If we, as parents, allow our children to be involved in a series of emotional relationships and permit "lite" physical relationships long before they are ready for marriage, we should not be surprised when our teens engage in full sexual intimacy.

It's a simple concept to grasp. If you want your kids to engage in premarital sex, let them get involved in emotional romance. Sex follows love. Premature, immature romantic love leads to premature, illicit sex. If you want to encourage your children (sons as well as daughters) to walk the aisle of their weddings as virgins, then help them develop a commitment to abstain from involvement in romantic relationships until they are ready to walk the aisle.

Postponing romance until you are ready to fulfill your romantic desires through the act of marriage is what courtship is all about. In my book *The Home Schooling Father*, I have written more extensively about how courtship works.

Virtually all of the parents I know who are home schooling their children were involved in dating. We were. You probably were as well. And as a consequence, the way we relate to others is often subtly tainted by our dating experience.

Dating trains young men and women to become commitment-breakers. Once the status of "boyfriend-girlfriend" has been achieved, a paper-thin commitment keeps them together—at least for a time. This is best described as the "I love you until . . ." promise, which can be translated, "I love you until someone cuter comes along and shows interest in me." Or, "I love you until I leave for college." Or, "I love you until I find someone richer, smarter, funnier, or who owns a nicer car." We learn a thousand excuses for breaking our commitment in the dating paradigm.

"Serial dating," as it has lately been termed, creates a societal atmosphere that makes it normal, acceptable, and understandable to "dump your honey" and find somebody new. We've all been through it. Most married home schooling parents went through this cycle countless times during their dating years. We followed Paul Simon's advice from his lyric, "There are fifty ways to leave your lover." Today it is not uncommon to have left fifty lovers (dating partners) along the way.

Societal acceptance of the dating paradigm has made "breaking up" not so hard to do. Breaking up over and over again with ill-suited dating partners creates habits that are fully transferred to marriage. No longer do most people really mean it when they say, "Till death do us part." Just as in their dating days, most people really mean, "I love you until...."

A married man is unlikely to dump his wife just because he meets a new woman who is marginally better looking than his wife. But let a woman who is far more attractive, younger, richer, who owns a red sports car come on the scene and begin flirtation, and he might suddenly change his loyalty, allegiance, and commitment.

When speaking to teens about dating, it's easy to illustrate how sticky the dating scene can be. Just pass around a roll of masking tape and have them tear off a strip long enough to make a loop. Ask the teens to take their tape and stick it on and pull it back off of whatever they want. It gets stuck to clothes, chairs, shoes, hair, the dirty floor, and anything in the room. After awhile the tape is really covered with dirt and is no longer very sticky. Ask the teens if the tape would do a very good job at holding up a poster. They will know the obvious answer is no!

Masking tape is a useful thing when it is fresh and new, but after it is has been stuck to so many other things, it loses much of its ability to bond to other surfaces. The problem with dating is that we are bonding and rebonding several times before we make our final selection. The rebonding process is like the masking tape. It gets soiled and loses its adhesiveness as the process goes on.

When God took one of Adam's ribs and created a wife for him, God set into motion an intimate bond between husband and wife. Adam looked at Eve and said, "This is now bone of my bones, and flesh of my flesh; she shall be called Woman, because she was taken out of Man" (Genesis 3:23). God instructed future husbands to "leave and cleave" in order to achieve "oneness" with their wives: "For this cause a man shall leave his father and his mother, and shall cleave to his wife; and they shall become one flesh" (Genesis 3:24). God established the bonding process from the very beginning of creation. Men and women were designed to bond to each other.

God created men and women to bond to their spouses on a physiological level as well as on an emotional level. Certain neurochemicals in our brains are released whenever we experience something that is pleasurable. When a couple "becomes one flesh" physically, the memory of the sexual experience is locked into the fabric of their minds. An invisible bond is formed between them. This bond makes their relationship different than any relationship they have.

When an unmarried couple has sex, an emotional and physical bond is also formed between them. When the couple goes their separate ways, the bond between them is damaged. Emotions are scarred in the process. The ability to fully bond to another might be difficult because they might naturally want to protect themselves against more pain.

As a marriage counselor, I (Reed) help many married couples work through past relationships that are affecting their present lives. People who had several dating partners can bring a lot of emotional baggage into their marriage. Those who have engaged in premarital sex add even more issues to deal with. It can be hard for a wife to trust her husband as the head of their home when he broke trust with God and her by engaging in premarital sex. It can also be difficult for a husband to respect his wife if she surrendered her virginity before marriage. What else would she give to get what she wants?

If your marriage is suffering from past mistakes you or your spouse made, do not despair. God is in the redemption business. Confess your mistakes to the Lord and seek His grace and forgiveness. He can give you a renewed mind and restore your marriage. He can make the tape sticky again.

Breaking the habits of heart and mind created by dating can only be done with God's help. If God's power can break other habits of sin, including physical addictions to drugs and alcohol, His power is more than sufficient to overcome this habit pattern as well.

Even though you are already married, the first step is to make the mental switch from the dating paradigm to the courtship paradigm. Realize that dating prepares you for divorce by developing habits that are fundamentally promiscuous. Courtship prepares you for marriage by creating habits that are fundamentally monogamous.

My own outlook was aided materially by developing courtship ideas for my children. As the thoughts of how I (Mike) wanted to train my own children in courtship germinated and grew, I realized how many old thought patterns still lurked in my mind. Adopting the idea of courtship for my own children has helped me gain victory over habits of mind developed by the dating experience.

Adverse Influence #3

Satan has an easier time attacking a marriage when one or both of the spouses have basic needs that are going unmet. Our old mental patterns of promiscuity developed in dating are more likely to reach a level of seriousness if we have current unmet needs in our marital relationship. An unmet need is never an excuse for any form of marital unfaithfulness—sexual or emotional—but unmet needs do create an atmosphere of greater risk for the person being tempted to give in to infidelity.

A man hungry for admiration will eat up words of praise from any source. If that source of admiration happens to be an attractive "other woman," he will be placed under an extra degree of temptation. If that same man receives regular praise and admiration from his wife, he is not nearly as likely to be subject to such a temptation. Likewise, wives who rarely receive words and acts of affection are much more likely to fall prey to gracious words of another man.

Our Desire for You

The purpose of this book is to help you understand the needs of your spouse. It is our desire that unmet needs will never be an issue that causes you or your spouse to give in to sexual or other temptation or to find yourselves on the brink of divorce. By learning how to meet your spouse's needs, we believe that you will develop an affair-proof, committed marriage that will last a lifetime. Five basic premises underlie our goal of helping you to meet the needs of your spouse:

1. Unmet needs are usually a contributing factor to marital unfaithfulness

Unmet needs are never an excuse for unfaithfulness, but we are kidding ourselves if we don't recognize that our failure to meet the needs of our spouses places extra pressure on them and decreases their ability to resist temptation.

Christians do not generally set out to have affairs. They usually say, "It just happened." But affairs do not just happen. A desire to look for love outside the marriage relationship is usually stimulated by unmet needs within the marriage. James 1:14-15 teaches, "But each one is tempted when, by his own evil desire, he is dragged away and enticed. Then, after desire has conceived, it gives birth to sin and sin, when it is full-grown, gives birth to death." A pastor once stated the principle more simply when he said, "Sin will take you farther than you want to go, let you stay longer than you want to stay, and make you pay more than you want to pay." A husband and wife give Satan a foothold in their marriage when they do not discover how to meet each other's needs.

2. Understanding and meeting the needs of your spouse is not optional

We do not have the luxury of saying, "He simply shouldn't stray," or "She simply should be a good wife." Blaming the other person—even when he or she is clearly in sin—does not excuse our failure to understand and meet the needs of our spouses.

3. Husbands must lead by example

If the husband meets his wife's needs, he creates an environment where the wife has a much easier time meeting his needs. A man who sincerely and consistently understands his wife's needs and takes action to meet those needs will almost invariably unlock a powerful force that will enable his wife to willingly and readily meet his needs.

If, for example, a husband provides his wife with consistent leadership (especially spiritual leadership), protection, and provision, she will have a much easier time giving her husband her approval and undying allegiance. When a husband properly shoulders his responsibilities, his wife is very likely to give a pleasing response.

4. Don't wait for your spouse to change

While the husband should be the leader, nevertheless, a wife is a fool if she waits for her husband to meet her needs before attempting to meet her husband's needs. Wives are simply living in fantasyland if they take the position that they will sit back and do nothing until their husbands begin to measure up. Husbands should take initiative, but a wife will find it in her own best interest to reinforce any small steps of improvement her husband makes with generous steps of her own.

5. We all need improvement

If you have any doubt of your need to improve, consider the following lists of the important needs of a home school wife and husband:

Important Needs of a Wife
- A wife needs her husband's *leadership.*
- A wife needs her husband to be *gentle* and *compassionate.*
- A wife needs her husband's *protection* and *provision.*
- A wife needs her husband's *active support* and *praise.*

Important Needs of a Husband
- A husband needs his wife's *allegiance.*
- A husband needs his wife's *affection* and *beauty*
- A husband needs his wife's *companionship* and *mature love*

These lists are not meant to be exhaustive, nor to suggest that a husband may not have some of the needs on the wife's list or vice versa. But in our interactions with home school families and Christians in general, we have observed that men and women have unique priorities of needs. We believe the needs we have listed above most often contribute to marital difficulties if they go unmet for a sustained period.

Our basic point is that we all need improvement. Put our lists to the acid test right now. Show the list of needs to your spouse and ask them to tell you if you are *perfect* in meeting all of these needs. Asking your spouse to show you your weak spots is tough. It takes courage and a willingness to be vulnerable. It is much easier to avoid and ignore problem areas, but detrimental to your marriage. I already asked my wife Vickie to whisper, "You are perfect," in my ear, and she politely exercised her Fifth Amendment right to remain silent.

We can all use improvement in our marriages. The stakes are so high. How can we hesitate? Our hope is that you will apply some of the information in this book and avoid some of the problems we have been seeing in home schoolers' marriages. Hosea 4:6 warns, "My people are destroyed from lack of knowledge." We trust that this book will provide you with some knowledge to help your marriage grow and prosper.

Don't allow your marriage to slip into the danger zone. Accept the challenge to meet the needs of your spouse, and you will reap the benefits of a satisfying love of a lifetime. A solid marriage will also keep the foundation for success with your children solid and unshaken.

Husbands, love your wives, just as Christ also loved the church and gave Himself up for her.

Ephesians 5:25

1

A WIFE NEEDS HER HUSBAND'S
Leadership

Attributes of Leadership
- A husband should lead his wife and children toward godliness
- A husband should make decisions that are wise and timely
- A husband should be a man of vision

*H*ave you ever heard of a Pushme-Pullyou? In one of Doctor Doolittle's adventures, he discovers a curious animal called the Pushme-Pullyou. It looks like a llama with a head and two front legs at each end. The two heads are always trying to go in opposite directions. They have a tough time getting anywhere.

The same is true in a family without the husband's leadership. The result is a two-headed family. If the husband won't lead, most women are forced to step up to the task to get things done. At times the two heads will be pulling in different directions because they are not focused on the same destination.

What direction is your home going? Who is leading that direction? The husband, wife, or even the children can be leading the home.

When I leave for work each day, I say in essence, "Honey, while I'm gone I give you the authority to raise our children in the manner we have agreed upon, to discipline as necessary, and to provide for their needs. When I return home, I will take that authority back from you and reassume my position of leadership." Even though the husband may not be in the home during the day, he can still maintain his leadership while he is away. The problem is that some dads don't reassume their position. They are content to let their wives carry the load.

God, however, did not design the family to work that way. God gave husbands the authority over the family (Ephesians 5, 1 Peter 3). He designated the husband to be the "head" of the home. With that authority comes the *responsibility* to lead.

In church we have heard the occasional sermon on how the wife is to be submissive to her husband. That is true, yet it wasn't designed to be a power struggle. Most wives are happy to follow if their husbands are willing to lead. In fact, if husbands love and lead as Christ did with tender yet courageous servant leadership, most wives will naturally submit to their husbands' authority.

When Janine and I (Reed) were first married, Janine paid our bills. Janine had lived on her own before we were married and had learned how to pay bills. My parents had taught me how to handle my money, manage a checking account, and save money, but they had never shown me how to pay bills. Since I had no experience at bill-paying, Janine took on the responsibility.

For several years the burden of managing our finances was on her shoulders. We always knew how much we were spending and where our money was going, but she took care of writing the checks and paying the bills on time. This put a fair amount of stress on her that increased over the years.

After several years and several children, it was more than she could keep up with. I began to take over the finances. Janine taught me the system, and we transitioned control. The key to our success was my desire to lead and my wife's grace and support. At times I made mistakes—some bills got paid late—but over all I learned how to lead in this area. I was not the only one learning about leadership. My wife had to learn how to let me lead.

Contrary to images created by the world around us, most Christian home schooling wives want their husbands to be the leaders in their homes. Most home schooling wives do not struggle with a temptation to take over as the leaders in their homes. Rather, if they have a problem it is usually a troubling dilemma created by their husbands' lack of leadership. Do they sit back and do nothing and let situations deteriorate while they wait for their husbands to lead? Or, do they step forward to fill the void and take charge of an issue?

Either alternative will never satisfy a wife who desires the biblical model for family living. She wants her husband to be active, to be involved, to be concerned. She wants her husband to get off his duff and lead.

Keep in mind our central premise—strong marriages are made when each spouse does his or her part to meet the needs of the other. Men, if your wife is a believer, she has a spiritual and emotional need for you to lead your family. Do it for her.

Consider the following attributes of leadership.

Spiritual Leadership

Spiritual leadership is the most important and most neglected aspect of a husband's responsibilities. When I (Mike) counsel husbands and wives, women often express their desire for their husbands to be the spiritual leaders in their homes. Men who are capable leaders on the job, in public life, and in church, are far too often slack when it comes to the spiritual leadership of their own families. Becoming the spiritual leader of our home is a lesson I have had to learn the hard way (and I am still learning).

My wife Vickie keeps a prayer journal in a small notebook. Her handwriting is very neat and tiny. (She can write an entire grocery list for a family of twelve on one medium-sized Post-It Note!) In just one journal, she has several years of weekly prayer requests. A few years ago, I peeked into her prayer notebook and was surprised to find that week after week, year upon year, her number one prayer request was "make Mike the spiritual leader in our home."

At the time I was reading her journal, I noticed that this request had been at a lower position on her list of prayer priorities for a number of months. I asked her if this meant that I was improving, and she said (in effect), "Improving? Yes. Lots of room for more improvement? Yes, again."

Many husbands, like me, struggle with spiritual leadership because it has been such a nebulous concept in our minds. We are told that we should be spiritual leaders. We are told we should take our family to church. We are told we should do family devotions. But that is about all of the instruction we have ever been given about spiritual leadership. I deal with this topic in depth in my book, *The Home Schooling Father*, but let's just review a few of the important principles of spiritual leadership right now.

A spiritual leader guides his wife and his children toward godliness. While this certainly includes activities such as church attendance and family devotions, we will fall sadly short of the mark if we equate these activities with the sum total of spiritual leadership.

True spiritual leadership involves three key attributes:
1. Setting spiritual goals
2. Planning activities and training designed to inculcate these goals
3. Periodically assessing progress

1. Set spiritual goals

Behind every successful business is a plan. Without a plan, a business will not survive for long. A successful manager works to reach the company's goals by training employees, evaluating the employees' success in meeting their goals, and then making necessary changes to the plan.

Our families' spiritual lives are more important than a business, so we should invest just as much energy making our families successful. Ideally, a husband should periodically sit down and assess his own spiritual status. He should note his strengths and his weaknesses. And he should set some new spiritual goals for himself that he hopes to achieve in the days and months ahead.

The first requirement of spiritual leadership is personal spiritual vitality. If you are not deliberately moving ahead in your own walk with God, you are going to have a difficult time leading others. The only time a true leader is frozen in place is after he is dead and a statue has been erected.

It is not enough to set goals for yourself and hope that your wife and children catch on by osmosis. Fathers should start with some basic spiritual goals for their family that are desirable for all born-again believers. Your goals may include helping them become familiar with the Bible, memorize Scripture, develop a prayer life, and learn how to share their faith and pray with someone who desires to become a Christian.

If you want spiritual fuzziness, don't set any goals. An old saying goes, "If you aim at nothing, you will hit it every time." If you want well-rounded spiritual maturity, then you need to begin with some precise goals that will allow you to hit precise targets.

But as your children get older, you should break out of the mold of setting your children's spiritual goals for them. By the time your children are in their mid-to-late teens, they should be setting their own goals. Your role as a father is to review these goals with them and to help them see spiritual blind spots or areas where their goals may not be a proper priority or doctrinally sound. In other words, you are an active advisor rather than a dictator in the later stages of your children's spiritual development. Your wife's chief concern and your main responsibility revolve around your desire to train children to be godly.

O.K., you may be thinking, "What does being a spiritual leader for my children have to do with meeting the needs of my wife?" One of the highest priorities in your wife's world is the spiritual nurturing of her children. When you actively engage in this process, she feels that your actions are demonstrating love toward *her*.

It took me (Mike) a long time to understand that this is more than a duty that I need to fulfill. Fulfilling my role as a spiritual leader for my children shows real love for my children, my wife, and God.

Spiritual leadership is not just about our children. Husbands and wives need to set their own spiritual goals as well. A husband and wife should also sit down periodically and go over an assessment of their own spiritual condition. A husband is either an egomaniac or a fool if he fails to ask his wife to review with him her observations concerning his own spiritual needs. Resistance may come from a husband because he is insecure or because his wife is simply being critical of him.

According to Proverbs 27:6, "Wounds from a friend can be trusted, but an enemy multiplies kisses." Our wives should be our best friends, having our best interests at heart. My wife is not going to criticize me just to tear me down. I value her observations. I want clear and specific information about my spiritual needs. I don't want someone who is just going to "kiss up" to me for various reasons. Other than God, who knows me better than my wife?

One of the keys to the Promise Keepers movement is accountability groups. We recognize the value when men gather together to bear one another's burdens and hold each other accountable. However, since my wife has more information on my true spiritual condition than anyone else does, I don't want to exclude her from providing input. "Better is an open rebuke than hidden love" (Proverbs 27:5).

Sometimes the truth hurts. I do not like the hurt, but I need to hear the truth. In reality my wife sometimes sees things that I miss. Just as "iron sharpens iron, so one man sharpens another" (Proverbs 27:17), my wife is helping me become more Christlike. Her insider's perspective can help me stay on God's path.

Dr. Richard Dobbins, one of my (Reed's) professors, once described marriage this way:

Love in a Christian marriage is a persistent effort on the part of two people to create for each other the circumstances in which each can become the person God intended for them to be, a better person than they could become alone.

You might need to read that again and let it sink in. Part of marriage is helping each other become more Christlike. Your job is not to change your spouse, but to help her become all that God desires her to be. Giving and receiving constructive criticism from time to time is necessary to bring about growth.

Let me assure you that your wife will feel that she is privileged to live in the home of a modern day biblical hero if you give her this kind of activist spiritual leadership that brims with order, purpose, and mutual accountability.

2. Plan activities that are designed to reach your goals

I have often struggled with family devotions. If I plan a devotion that is suitable for my older children, then my younger kids are "left in the dust." If I try to speak on a level the younger children can understand, then my older kids are bored. I have yet to find the "magic solution" to this dilemma in the context of devotions, but I have realized that devotions are not the only method of training my children in godliness.

The older-younger devotions dilemma is solvable only when you realize that devotions are only one component of spiritual training. Scripture tells us to disciple our children throughout the day in a variety of ways:

> And you shall teach them [God's commands] diligently to your sons and shall talk of them when you sit in your house and when you walk by the way and when you lie down and when you rise up. (Deuteronomy 6:7 NASB)

In addition to family devotions, we should plan individual activities for our children's spiritual development that are consistent with the goals we have established.

If we want our children to become effective witnesses, for example, we can help our children memorize salvation verses, write their personal testimony, learn how to present the gospel in an organized manner, practice a salvation presentation, or learn how to use both Scripture and logic to answer common questions from unbelievers.

Some spiritual training can be integrated into devotions. But some training will require one-on-one time with your children. When you have designed a broad program of spiritual training, you need not worry if devotions are not pitched at an ideal level for your whole family. In our family devotions I try to use devotional material that will keep the interest of my youngest children and add comments of a more mature level that will spark the older children's interest.

Ideally (and I have a hard time living up to this ideal myself) family devotions could be a part of an integrated plan that focuses on a particular theme. Using the evangelism example once again, you could read Bible stories on salvation and evangelism for one week, memorize salvation verses a second week, have older children share their testimony a third week, and pray for unsaved friends throughout the time that your family is focusing on evangelism.

3. Periodically assess progress

Reviewing the goals you have made and evaluating your progress will help you and your family stay on track. You can sit down perhaps once a month with your wife and each child one-on-one. You can review the spiritual goals that were the focus of the past month's activities, talk about insights gained in personal devotions, and give advice on further steps of needed follow-through. When you and your wife discuss your younger children's progress, keep in mind their ages, stages of development, and levels of maturity. Some goals will take more time to reach than others will. Each child will learn at a different rate.

Any wife who desires her husband to be the spiritual leader of her home will be thrilled if he undertakes any portion of these ideas to increase the effectiveness of his spiritual leadership. Your wife will feel loved and cared for by your actions to lead your family in godliness.

I (Reed) have yet to read a survey or study that measured how spiritual leadership impacts a marriage, but I see the evidence each day in my office as husbands and wives share with me how effective spiritual leadership has strengthened their marriages.

Happy, healthy marriages have husbands who lead spiritually.

Decisive Leadership

Many men have a difficult time making good decisions. Some flounder because they lack wisdom. Decisions are made that are shortsighted or based on wrong information. Others will make snap decisions without proper reflection and research, while some, frozen by fear or given to laziness, will simply refuse to make any decision. Then circumstances or time will make the decision for them.

Acts 15:1-31 gives us an example of how the early church leaders made decisions. Paul and Barnabas had just returned from their first missionary journey. A dispute arose over whether the new Gentile believers had to be circumcised or not and how "Jewish" did they need to become to be accepted by the church. Paul and Barnabas traveled to Jerusalem to meet with the church leaders to present the circumcision dilemma. The church leaders discussed the issue, came up with a solution, and sent Paul and Barnabas away with a letter to all the churches explaining the solution.

Here is a formula for biblical decision making:

Define the problem

In Acts 15, the church leaders first clarified the issue. They made sure they were all addressing the same problem.

Often my wife and I (Reed) can be talking about the same subject but coming from two different views. Until we get on the same wavelength, we can become frustrated with each other, which can lead us downhill quickly to an argument. We have learned from experience to define our goal and the problem or topic at the beginning of our discussion.

Discuss ways of solving the problem

The disciples talked about what they could do. They discussed the matter thoroughly.

At this step my wife and I list all of our options or potential solutions. We brainstorm for awhile. We do not allow ourselves to critique or criticize each other's ideas. Verbal or nonverbal criticism of your spouse's ideas at this time may cause her to pull out of the conversation. A frustrated or hurt spouse saying, "Do whatever you want; I don't care," is not *carte blanche* to make the decision your own way. So hold off on critiquing possibilities until the next step. Right now just think of potential solutions.

Decide on the best possible option

The apostles had a long list from the "Law of Moses" for solutions to their problem. They narrowed the possibilities down to four.

At this step my wife and I discuss the pros and cons of our potential solutions. Our goal is to come up with a workable plan. The focus is not simply trying to sway the other's opinion to satisfy our personal desires. We try to answer the question: What are we going to do about it? The emphasis is on *we*, not me.

Summarize the plan you come up with so everyone clearly understands the direction you are going together

The apostles wrote a letter that they sent with Paul and Barnabas that listed the four requirements for fellowship among the Jewish and Gentile believers.

This step can easily be overlooked, but when used it can help you avoid misunderstandings that can lead to conflict. For example, a couple works through the first three steps of the decision but skips the fourth. At one point they begin to branch off into separate directions. The dialogue sounds like this:

"Honey, what are you doing?"

"I'm following the suggestions we talked about."

"No, you're not. We talked about that but later decided to do this step the other way."

"Oh, you're right! I forgot that change. I'm sorry. Let me start again."

This is the ideal way to handle a miscommunication. But what really happens often sounds like this:

"Hey! What are you doing? I knew you were going to do your own thing. You never want to follow the plan. You always have your own agenda. Fine—I will do it my way!"

This couple continues on in separate directions, and unity is lost. The simple step of summarizing the steps involved in the solution helps to eliminate any misunderstandings before you begin. You then begin *and* finish together.

My goal as the leader in my home is to make decisions that are best for everyone involved, not what is easiest for me. Unity in our home comes from serving others even as we lead. At times I make a decision that, in my opinion, seems to be the longer route to our goal. If I did not have to consider my family, I would take a shorter path. Our goal is to get there together, and not to lose some of the family along the way. Bypassing the quickest route can be hard for men to do sometimes, but a good leader always looks out for the best interests of those under his care before his own.

Working with your wife to make decisions can seem at odds with our need to be decisive. Yes, leaders make decisions. And you cannot meet your wife's need for leadership if you refuse to come to a conclusion. But you cannot win your wife's confidence unless you consult with her and give her views great weight in your evaluation. In nearly thirty years of marriage, I (Mike) have never made a major decision without Vickie's active involvement and enthusiastic approval. Her input has been beneficial and valued. Sometimes I have made decisions on my own concerning issues that I thought were minor, but even in these matters I would have been well-advised to talk with my wife first.

Leadership at times is a balancing act. You are to serve your family, yet at the same time lead. Here is a poem by H. Gordon Selfridge that captures the dilemma of leadership:

No Extremes in Leadership

Self-reliant but not Self-sufficient
Energetic but not Self-seeking
Steadfast but not Stubborn

Tactful but not Timid
Serious but not Sullen
Loyal but not Sectarian

Unmovable but not Stationary
Gentle but not Hypersensitive
Tenderhearted but not Touchy

Conscientious but not a Perfectionist
Disciplined but not Demanding
Generous but not Gullible
Meek but not Weak
Humorous but not Hilarious
Friendly but not Familiar

Holy but not Holier-than-thou
Discerning but not Critical
Progressive but not Pretentious[1]

Visionary Leadership

When Vickie and I (Mike) began to realize that we wanted to spend the rest of our lives together, one of our most frequent topics of conversation was "the future." Our decision to get married was strongly influenced by the fact that our goals for the future were so much in harmony. We dreamed together about how we wanted our lives to turn out, and we were willing to work together to accomplish those dreams.

It is widely recognized that women have a strong desire for security in their lives. A woman's sense of security is dramatically enhanced when she believes that her husband has a life plan and is working according to this plan in the major areas of his life. This does not mean that a man's plan for his life won't ever change. When Vickie and I married, we never talked about home schooling because we had never heard about it. We did not agree on having a very large family. In fact, while we were together in college, I won a speech contest advocating zero population growth. We had no plans to move to Virginia. All of these plans came later as God revealed new paths for us to take.

We did plan how I would become a lawyer. We did agree that my purpose in becoming a lawyer would be to advance godly principles. We did agree on having children and that Vickie would stay home with our children. Very early in our marriage we agreed that we would give our children a Christian education. We also talked and dreamed about future involvement in politics.

The details have changed—some dramatically. But the big picture is, for the most part, quite consistent with the general plans we made together in the months before our marriage.

Most couples dream these kinds of dreams prior to marriage. But they fail to keep the dreams alive, updated, modified, and fresh. It is easy after children come along for all of our attention, dreams, and energy to be focused on them. Home schoolers are particularly guilty of this. Besides just raising our children, we have taken on the responsibility of educating them.

A healthy marriage reserves, even guards time, for the husband and wife to continue their dreams and relationship. Couples who focus all their attention on their children can end up not knowing each other after the children are raised and gone. That is a difficult place to be. For those couples who do not want to get to know each other again, divorce may be the end result.

When a husband or wife begins to become a lesser priority than all the other demands of life, including the raising of children, the couple's marriage can be placed at risk. The spouse who feels neglected begins to look elsewhere for someone to talk to or for someone who will listen. When someone else begins to meet those needs, Satan has found a foothold in the marriage. Temptation may seem too difficult to overcome.

One of the things that is important to do as you take the time to keep your marriage fresh and alive is to revisit your old dreams. Update them. Converge them. But spend the time it takes to build a unity of vision between husband and wife.

But at some point a husband must do more than talk about dreams; he must make them happen. A wife will eventually become disillusioned if her husband is "all talk and no action." She will have a strong temptation to label her husband a "dreamer" or just plain lazy if he fails to pursue the life plans they have dreamed together.

Dreams build hopes, which are eventually dashed if there is never any progress toward the goal.

Developing a "Problem Solver's Vision"

To lead our families, we need to be men of vision. But sometimes the term *vision* seems to imply things that are far off, even remote. One very practical meaning of *vision* is *the ability to see stuff.* The kind of vision that is critical to meeting the needs of your wife involves seeing a problem and then having the necessary insight to find a creative solution. In order to "see" a problem, you first have to pay attention to the circumstances that surround you.

I (Mike) have started a number of organizations—Home School Legal Defense Association, Patrick Henry College, the Madison Project, our church, and a few others. People recognize this as leadership. But every one of these organizations has come through a process of thinking that is fully applicable to leading a family. For each one, I saw a problem or an unmet need and figured out a creative solution. (I fully give God the credit for whatever ability I possess and for specific insights.) The ability to see your wife's unmet needs or to understand problems she faces, and then to be able to find creative solutions is a real asset that you can bring to your marriage.

I have learned to read my wife's emotional status with a fair degree of accuracy. If she is showing signs of burnout, I move into the "I'm going to take over for you" mode of action. I will make dinner or bring home a pizza so I can help relieve her stress. Throughout the evening I try to take as much of the load of raising ten children as possible. When things are all settled down, we go for a one-hour walk. On this walk, my goal is to let Vickie talk about her troubles. My job is just to listen and provide encouragement.

As men we have a difficult time listening without prematurely trying to solve the problem. Wives often share their problems with us for the relief that sharing brings—not because they desire a solution. We need to first listen to our wives and only give answers if she thinks a problem still exists when she is through talking it out.

Most men and women lack listening skills. Everyone desires to be heard, but rarely do people desire to listen. As someone is talking, we are thinking about what we are going to say next or what we want to eat for dinner. Listening well does not come naturally. It is a skill that must be practiced and fine-tuned. Here are some simple skills that will help you improve your listening:

1. *Listen completely.* We often assume we know what our spouse is going to say, so rather than listening we work on our response. This works only as long as we guess correctly. If we guess incorrectly, we might be in for a "discussion" about how we never listen. To avoid letting your thoughts wander, look your spouse in the eye as she is talking and you will not be as distracted by your own thoughts.

2. *Summarize what your spouse says.* After your spouse shares with you some problems she is facing, you might summarize her thoughts. But it is probably best to

do this subtly rather than to use mechanical repetition. For example, I (Mike) think it is better to say, "Yeah, I really understand how the boys' behavior is frustrating," rather than, "You appear to be frustrated with the boys." Both versions show that you heard her, but the first version shows that you also understand. Sometimes I just let her know I'm listening by simple comments such as "that's interesting" or "I never looked at it that way." Summarizing what your spouse tells you reassures her that you are listening and gives her an opportunity to clarify her meaning.

3. *Allow the listener adequate time to respond.* After your spouse has listened completely to you, allow him or her extra time to respond to you. If your spouse was listening to you attentively, he or she will need time to think through a response. Practice patience. My wife and I (Reed) call these pregnant pauses. These pauses, like pregnancy, will come to an end, but I do not always know when. Also, like pregnancy, the longer it goes on, the more uncomfortable it gets. So be patient.

4. *Reduce any distractions.* It is important to give your undivided attention to each other. Distractions can bring frustration, which can lead to anger. When I (Reed) come home from work, I like to listen to how my wife's day went and tell her about my day. If my children interrupt us several times while she is talking to me, I have a hard time listening. I can try hard to listen, but the interruptions are frustrating. I become angry because I am trying to listen to her, but I can't with all that is going on at that time.

When I sense the frustration building because of so many distractions, I usually handle the problem one of two ways. First, I ask the children not to interrupt. I tell them, "This is Dad and Mom's time to talk." Or, I table the discussion with my wife. I might say, "Honey, there are a lot of distractions right now, and I am having a hard time listening to you. Can we continue this conversation in the kitchen after dinner or after we put the children to bed?"

Being a visionary leader means understanding the needs of your wife and meeting those needs in the big problem areas as well as the small "everyday" situations. Whether the circumstances are great or small, every time you show your concern by observing what is going on in your wife's life and then demonstrating wisdom by meeting her needs, you will prove yourself to be the kind of husband your wife has always dreamed of—a man of real vision.

Lot's Legacy of Leadership

Historical episodes recorded in Scripture teach us a variety of biblical principles. Some stories demonstrate the blessings that come from obeying God. Other stories demonstrate the consequences of disobeying God. The story of Lot teaches the consequences of failing to be a leader for one's family.

Lot started out toward Sodom and Gomorrah because he selfishly chose the greener pasturelands when his Uncle Abraham gave him a choice. He ended up living in the city and even acquired a leader's position of influence. Genesis 19:1 records that Lot sat in the gate of Sodom. Those who "sat in the gate" were the rulers and leaders of ancient cities. Even though Lot held a position of authority, he did not lead others toward righteousness. He had reached a comfortable compromise with sin. Lot sat in the gate, but failed to lead as God intended.

When Abraham learned of Sodom and Gomorrah's coming destruction, he pleaded with God to spare the city if there were just ten righteous in it. But there were not, and the city was destroyed.

Could there have been ten righteous? Let's just count up Lot's immediate family: (1) Lot, (2) Mrs. Lot, (3) Daughter #1, (4) Daughter #2. Each daughter was engaged, so this adds (5) Fiancé #1, (6) Fiancé #2. Each fiancé had parents, so this adds (7), (8), (9), and (10). If Lot had simply reached the members of his own family and in-laws, then Sodom and Gomorrah would have escaped God's judgment.

Lot's wife didn't even escape God's wrath. She was so addicted to the life of sin that she turned and looked back at the city and permanently became a pillar in her community. Lot failed to lead his wife in righteousness and the consequences were fatal.

Lot failed to lead his daughters in righteousness as well. Of course, Lot did offer his daughters to the mob of perverts who demanded to have sex with Lot's angelic visitors. Later these poor girls were so mixed up that they believed the best way to preserve the heritage of their family was to get their father drunk and get pregnant by their father. As a result, Lot's older daughter conceived a son that was later named Moab, the father of the nation known as the Moabites. Lot's younger daughter conceived a son later named Ben-Ammi, who became the father of the Ammonites.

Lot's lack of leadership had devastating results for many generations. During the Israelites' exodus from Egypt, the men of Israel were drawn to Baal worship at Peor, committing sexual sins with Moabite women (Numbers 25). The Israelites were also enticed to worship the god Molech, who was a god of the Ammonites. Generation after generation provoked God as they bowed to Baal and worshipped Molech instead of Yahweh. Scripture records that even Solomon was guilty of sacrificing to the gods of the Moabites and Ammonites.

> On a hill east of Jerusalem, Solomon built a high place for Chemosh the detestable god of Moab, and for Molech the detestable god of the Ammonites. (1 Kings 11:7)

God's disappointment in His chosen people is clearly displayed when Jeremiah delivered God's message to the Israelites:

> They built high places for Baal in the Valley of Ben Hinnom to sacrifice their sons and daughters to Molech, though I never commanded, nor did it enter My mind, that they should do such a detestable thing and so make Judah sin. (Jeremiah 32:35)

Child sacrifices with the Ammonites and sexual sin with the Moabites were the legacy of Lot, the man who neglected the spiritual leadership of his family. It doesn't take a great imagination to suggest that a man of today who fails to lead his family may find his children in the same predicament. Children who become involved in sexual sin may eventually give up their own children to the modern form of child sacrifice—abortion.

If we place a high value on our children and desire to leave a righteous legacy, then genuine leadership is not optional; it is the fundamental duty of every Christian father. Lot's example serves as a serious reminder of the penalty if we fail to lead.

Hindrances to Leadership

Lot may have suffered from some other major hindrances to leadership as well, such as laziness, fear, selfishness, and busyness.

Laziness

Laziness is a habit antithetical to good leadership. A godly leader will not squander the resources of time or energy at his disposal. I (Mike) greatly appreciate the analogy I learned from Gregg Harris. He taught me that if we treat each hour of the day as a $100 bill that we have to spend that hour, we can quickly learn how to accumulate the real treasures that only time can buy. If we spend our $2,400 a day on junk, what will we have to show after a year or after ten years? But if we spend our

$2,400 a day on investments of time that will last, we will look back on the passing years as a man wealthy in the things that only time wisely invested can buy.

Fear

Some men are not good leaders because they are paralyzed by fear. Godly caution is an excellent attribute, but fear is the misuse of this tendency. Fear normally arises when a man is overly concerned about himself and too little concerned with serving others and obeying God. Paul encouraged Timothy to fear not when he said, "For God hath not given us the spirit of fear; but of power, and of love, and of a sound mind" (2 Timothy 1:7 KJV). The enemy uses fear to paralyze us. When fears hold us captive, indecision rules. God wants us to rest in His peace and His love for us. Remember fear's origin: "There is no fear in love. But perfect love drives out fear, because fear has to do with punishment. The one who fears is not made perfect in love" (1 John 4:7).

Selfishness

Selfishness is the bane of our times. Our culture teaches us to look out for "number one" above all others. Leadership in the home, God's style, demands a selfless spirit.

In C.S. Lewis's delightful allegorical novels, *The Chronicles of Narnia*, King Lune (a central character in *The Horse and His Boy*) describes the selfless heart of a true leader to his long-lost son who has just discovered that he will someday become king:

For this is what it means to be a king: to be first in every desperate attack and last in every desperate retreat, and when there's hunger in the land (as must be now and then in bad years) to wear finer clothes and laugh louder over a scantier meal than any man in your land.[2]

Leadership is about being a servant and laying down your life for your family.

Busyness

Finally, a leader should never be distracted from his responsibilities by ordinary busyness.

I (Mike) have a jar full of rice and walnuts—three large walnuts. If I empty the jar and try to place the rice in first and then the walnuts, the walnuts protrude from the top, and the lid simply will not fit. But if I put the big walnuts in first, and then pour in the rice, everything fits perfectly.

The walnuts symbolize the major priorities of my life. One walnut is my relationship with God. The second walnut is my relationship with my wife, and the third walnut is my relationship with my children. If I schedule my priorities (the walnuts) first, the rice (which symbolizes all the clutter of a busy life) will easily fit in around my priorities. If some things just don't fit in, it is far better to lose a few grains of rice, than to be unable to take care of my "walnuts"—life's true priorities.

Take time to schedule real priority time with your wife and children. Do not let the busyness of life rob you of your richest reward.

Leaders Versus Bosses

H. Gordon Selfridge built up one of the world's largest department stores in London. He achieved success by being a leader, not a boss. Here is his comparison of the two types of executives:

> The boss drives his men; the leader coaches them.
> The boss depends upon authority; the leader on good will.
> The boss inspires fear; the leader inspires enthusiasm.
> The boss says "I;" the leader, "We."
> The boss fixes the blame for the breakdown; the leader fixes the breakdown.
> The boss knows how it is done; the leader shows how.
> The boss says "Go;" the leader says, "Let's go!"[3]

Leadership demands your constant attention to the needs of your wife and your family. The price is high, but the reward is priceless. When you fully accept the mantle of leadership that God has asked you to accept, your family will have a righteous legacy for generations to come.

Notes

1. H. Gordon Selfridge, "Leaders Versus Bosses," in Paul Lee Tan, *Encyclopedia of 7700 Illustrations* (Rockville, MD: Assurance Publishers, 1979), 719.
2. C.S. Lewis, *The Horse and His Boy* (New York, NY: Scholastic Inc, 1954), 215.
3. H. Gordon Selfridge, 720.

For where you go, I will go, and where you stay, I will stay. Your people will be my people, and your God, my God.

Ruth 1:16b

2

A HUSBAND NEEDS HIS WIFE'S
Allegiance

Attributes of Allegiance
- A wife should give approval to her husband
- A wife should encourage her husband to change by encouragement not criticism
- A wife should be loyal to her husband

*T*he flip-side of a wife's need for her husband's leadership is the man's need for his wife's allegiance. O.K., we're a couple of guys writing this book, so we can be brutally honest about our own gender. Men have big, big ego needs that only their wives can legitimately fill.

We need a woman to think that we are great. We need a woman to think that we do great things.

On the surface this may seem petty and self-centered. And at times men certainly behave in such ways. But there is a proper place for this need as well.

For those of us who are building our lives on the traditional biblical assumptions about the roles of husbands and wives, we believe that a man has a tremendous responsibility to engage the world outside the home for the benefit of his family. This is done primarily through his role as the breadwinner for the family.

Would the reader allow me (Mike) a disclaimer? Because I am involved in politics, people read my books to find little snippets that they can use to harass me. I know that expressing traditional ideas about the role of men and women will be one of the passages my critics will scour looking for juicy quotes. So let me talk to such people for just one paragraph.

Note to political scouts and other cultural liberals reading this book: I know this sounds hopelessly out of date to "modern" ears. If you disagree, fine—go watch some Allen Alda reruns and get a dose of a style more to your liking. We are writing this book for those who *want* to live according to the Bible. We do not suggest that anyone should be forced to live according to God's plan for marriage. We think that people will be happier if they obey God, but we wouldn't dream of using political power to coerce you to follow our views on the best approach for family life.

O.K., back to the task at hand.

As men engage the world through their jobs, there is a real sense of competition and at times a fairly desperate struggle for survival. In the midst of such activity, there is a deep and legitimate need for a man to have the security of knowing that at least one person in this world is faithfully on his side.

Several years ago, there was a popular song "You and Me Against the World" by Helen Ready. Even though the song was about the relationship between a mom and her child, the lyrics can also be applied to a husband-wife relationship. Men need the love-based approval that the lyrics of that song suggest. We need to come home to find a woman who will make us believe that we have her deep admiration. A man needs his wife to believe that he is talented, good-looking, fundamentally good, and at least on his way to success.

Sometimes men give their wives a real challenge to believe such things. Women who are able to give their unflinching approval to their husbands—despite what would appear to the outside world some obvious short-comings—perform great acts of love.

A wise wife finds a basis for hope and believes in her husband's future. She believes in him—either as he is or as he will be in "just a little while." The apostle Paul got it just right when he wrote that love "bears all things, believes all things, hopes all things, endures all things" (1 Corinthians 13:7 NKJV).

Giving your husband approval has many facets. But before we turn to our detailed discussion, let me say what approval is *not*. Approval does not require a wife to agree with everything her husband says and does. Approval means that when you disagree, you graciously believe that he will get it right the next time.

General Versus Specific Approval

A wife's approval can be general or specific. General approval sounds like this: "Honey, you're the greatest! You're the best!" It's open-ended. Specific approval is, at times, much more powerful. For example, when you say, "Honey, I really appreciate the way you pay our bills on time," your husband will know exactly what he did that made you happy. Or when you say to your husband, "You know, our yard really looks great. Thanks for mowing it," he will know exactly what you appreciate.

Specific approval recognizes a task, trait, or action that you like. If you are having difficulty giving approval to your husband, look more specifically at all he does for you. What originally attracted you to him? What does he do for you that you take for granted? You might surprise your husband when he gets home from work by saying, "Honey, I really appreciate the way you go to work everyday to provide for our family." He will be delighted to hear you voice your appreciation after he's had a difficult day on the job.

Heavenly Approval

God designed human beings to need approval. As Christians we spend our whole earthly lives working to please our Heavenly Father as we await that day when we will meet Him face to face. I am not implying that we have to earn our way into heaven—salvation is a free gift—but we do strive to become more Christlike (Galatians 2:20) and to follow the Father's will (Luke 2:49).

When I get to heaven, I may marvel at the streets of pure gold that are clear as glass, or I may be amazed at the beauty of heavenly mansions. But surpassing those things will be the words of approval and encouragement I want to and need to hear from the Lord. More than anything else I desire to hear Him say, "Well done thou good and faithful servant" (Matthew 25:23). My spirit will rejoice, "Ahhh…I did a good job! The Lord approves of my efforts." I will enjoy hearing those words. I will cherish them.

We all have a need to be approved, and we work to gain that approval. Wives, your approval of your husbands helps to satisfy that need.

Motivating Change

Your encouraging words of approval also help bring about change in your husband. Change can happen one of two ways, by criticism or by encouragement. Criticism will bring about change, but it has its limits. When people are routinely criticized, they will change for a period of time until they get fed up with the criticism and give up trying. When their patience is worn thin, they will react by saying, "That's it! I'm not changing another thing. I don't care what the consequences from you are. I've had it. I can't stand anymore of this." Criticism, at this point, loses its ability to motivate change in others.

Attempting to motivate changes in people through criticism may also discourage the right attitude. You may get them to perform the behavior you want, but they will have an "attitude" while they do it. They may mumble under their breath, give you the silent treatment, or show their true feelings through nonverbal communication such as glaring looks, slamming doors, or banging things around. One family I (Reed) worked with knew it was time to back off their demands of Mom when they heard the kitchen cupboards slamming while she was cooking. If we want genuine change with a joyful spirit, criticism is not the way to get it.

The best way to motivate changes in your spouse is through encouragement and approval. When your husband does something right, tell him! Often we only verbalize what others are doing wrong. Husbands sometimes stumble onto something their wives like, but without hearing approval from their wives the chances of them repeating it are slim. Your encouragement reinforces that it is a job well done. Without your approval he has no idea how you feel.

You can encourage change even when you may not see much improvement happening. For instance, let's say your husband helped your son with a math question. You might encourage him by saying, "Honey, I really appreciate the way you help with the children's school work." All he may have done was answer one question for one of your children, but letting him know what you appreciate will encourage him to do that action again. People are more likely to live up to someone's positive

expectations of them rather than try to change someone's negative perspective of them.

Your relationship with your husband may be
strained for several reasons. You may feel frustrated
because your husband isn't doing much to help with
home schooling, or he may not be much help with anything around the house, or... (you can fill in the blank).
As your frustration mounts, your mind only comes up
with advice you want to give your husband—not praise.

One couple I (Reed) counseled had let their frustra-
tions with each other drive a wedge between them. The
wife had become resentful toward her husband because
of his lack of involvement in the home. Her anger
toward him had made it difficult for her to see anything
good in him. Faults and shortcomings were all she could
see at that point.

I encouraged her to give her husband verbal
approval. She knew this would take some mental creativity on her part, but she agreed to try. She thought
about what she could say and came up with, "Honey, I
appreciate the way you go to work everyday and provide
for us." Another time she told him, "It really blesses me
the way you are home in the evening instead of being
over-involved in other things outside the home." She
had to look past her frustration that all he did in the
evening was sit on the couch and watch TV or play
games on the computer.

As she continued to praise him for what he did right,
he began to change. He told her that for a long time he
had felt that all he was to the family was a paycheck and

an outsider. Her approval began to draw him in. He began to feel secure enough to address his lack of involvement and to engage in meaningful change.

Pure Allegiance

A wife demonstrates allegiance to her husband by being loyal to him in her words, her actions, and her dreams. Ruth is a woman in Scripture who stands out for her loyalty. After her husband died, her mother-in-law, Naomi, gave her permission to go back to her family and find a husband. Ruth's allegiance to Naomi was communicated beautifully:

> But Ruth replied, "Don't urge me to leave you or to turn back from you. Where you go I will go, and where you stay I will stay. Your people will be my people and your God my God. Where you die I will die, and there I will be buried. May the Lord deal with me, be it ever so severely, if anything but death separates you and me." (Ruth 1:16-17)

The Lord blessed Ruth's allegiance to Naomi. As she returned with Naomi to Bethlehem, the Lord provided for their needs during a time of famine through the generosity of the wealthy landowner, Boaz. Ruth once again showed her faithful allegiance to Naomi when she followed Naomi's instructions in regards to seeking Boaz's attention. Boaz recognized Ruth's noble character, and he became her kinsman-redeemer (her husband). Naomi was honored as a result of Ruth and Boaz's union:

The women said to Naomi: "Praise be to the
Lord, who this day has not left you without a
kinsman-redeemer. May he become famous
throughout Israel! He will renew your life and
sustain you in your old age. For your daughter-
in-law, who loves you and who is better to you
than seven sons, has given him birth."

Then Naomi took the child, laid him in her lap
and cared for him. The women living there said,
"Naomi has a son." And they named him Obed.
He was the father of Jesse, the father of David.
(Ruth 4:14-17)

God not only blessed Ruth with a child and Naomi
with a grandchild, but also He allowed them to be a part
of the Messiah's family tree. Through the line of Obed,
and on to David, kings would be born and ultimately,
the King of Kings.

God honored Ruth's allegiance and her noble character. Ruth modeled for all women how to be loyal. She
was willing to follow her mother-in-law to the ends of
the earth if she had to. In unstable times Ruth did not
say, "See ya, Naomi. I think I can do better on my own."
She respected Naomi's leadership and vowed her undying allegiance.

When times get tough, do you remain loyal to your
husband's leadership? Or do you begin doubting him
and second-guessing his actions? Do you want to take
the reins and try to solve your family's problems on your
own?

Ruth accepted Naomi's instructions to lie at Boaz's feet on the threshing floor. She could have said, "Naomi, you are crazy. I'm not going to do such a risky thing as that. What would people think?" Instead, she obeyed Naomi's instructions explicitly, and God blessed her for it.

Your husband will feel respected and honored if you show him the kind of loyalty that Ruth had toward Naomi. He will be empowered to lead when you allow him to be in charge by trusting his judgment. Your trust will give him confidence to take the reins and do what he feels is best for you and your family.

Abigail's Allegiance

Another story from Scripture shows allegiance in another light. Consider the story of Abigail and Nabal.

Now Samuel died, and all Israel assembled and mourned for him; and they buried him at his home in Ramah.

Then David moved down into the Desert of Maon. A certain man in Maon, who had property there at Carmel, was very wealthy. He had a thousand goats and three thousand sheep, which he was shearing in Carmel. His name was Nabal and his wife's name was Abigail. She was an intelligent and beautiful woman, but her husband, a Calebite, was surly and mean in his dealings.

While David was in the desert, he heard that Nabal was shearing sheep. So he sent ten young men and said to them, "Go up to Nabal at Carmel and greet him in my name. Say to him: 'Long life to you! Good health to you and your household! And good health to all that is yours!

"'Now I hear that it is sheep-shearing time. When your shepherds were with us, we did not mistreat them, and the whole time they were at Carmel nothing of theirs was missing. Ask your own servants and they will tell you. Therefore be favorable toward my young men, since we come at a festive time. Please give your servants and your son David whatever you can find for them.'"

When David's men arrived, they gave Nabal this message in David's name. Then they waited.

Nabal answered David's servants, "Who is this David? Who is this son of Jesse? Many servants are breaking away from their masters these days. Why should I take my bread and water, and the meat I have slaughtered for my shearers, and give it to men coming from who knows where?"

David's men turned around and went back. When they arrived, they reported every word. David said to his men, "Put on your swords!" So they put on their swords, and David put on his. About four hundred men went up with David, while two hundred stayed with the supplies.

One of the servants told Nabal's wife Abigail: "David sent messengers from the desert to give our master his greetings, but he hurled insults at them. Yet these men were very good to us. They did not mistreat us, and the whole time we were out in the fields near them nothing was missing. Night and day they were a wall around us all the time we were herding our sheep near them. Now think it over and see what you can do, because disaster is hanging over our master and his whole household. He is such a wicked man that no one can talk to him."

Abigail lost no time. She took two hundred loaves of bread, two skins of wine, five dressed sheep, five seahs of roasted grain, a hundred cakes of raisins and two hundred cakes of pressed figs, and loaded them on donkeys. Then she told her servants, "Go on ahead; I'll follow you." But she did not tell her husband Nabal.

As she came riding her donkey into a mountain ravine, there were David and his men descending toward her, and she met them. David had just said, "It's been useless—all my watching over this fellow's property in the desert so that nothing of his was missing. He has paid me back evil for good. May God deal with David, be it ever so severely, if by morning I leave alive one male of all who belong to him!"

When Abigail saw David, she quickly got off her donkey and bowed down before David with her face to the ground. She fell at his feet and said: "My lord, let the blame be on me alone. Please let your servant speak to you; hear what your servant has to say. May my lord pay no attention to that wicked man Nabal. He is just like his name—his name is Fool, and folly goes with him. But as for me, your servant, I did not see the men my master sent.

"Now since the Lord has kept you, my master, from bloodshed and from avenging yourself with your own hands, as surely as the Lord lives and as you live, may your enemies and all who intend to harm my master be like Nabal. And let this gift, which your servant has brought to my master, be given to the men who follow you. Please forgive your servant's offense, for the Lord will certainly make a lasting dynasty for my master, because he fights the Lord's battles. Let no wrongdoing be found in you as long as you live. Even though someone is pursuing you to take your life, the life of my master will be bound securely in the bundle of the living by the Lord your God. But the lives of your enemies he will hurl away as from the pocket of a sling. When the Lord has done for my master every good thing he promised concerning him and has appointed him leader over Israel, my master will not have on his conscience the staggering burden of needless bloodshed or of having avenged himself. And when the Lord has brought my master success, remember your servant." (1 Samuel 25:1-31)

Like many stories in Scripture, we can learn not only from positive examples like Ruth and Naomi, but we can also learn from negative examples such as Abigail, Nabal, and David.

Abigail is a classic example of a woman in need of her husband's leadership. Her husband was about to let death come upon all the men in his household because of his stubbornness and selfishness. His lack of leadership caused Abigail to take action. She saved her husband's neck by disregarding his wishes and taking charge. Her husband should have done the right thing by taking care of the men who had taken care of him, but he was too foolish to realize what threatening circumstances they were in. Although no contract existed between David and Nabal, David's labor should have been rewarded because Nabal's assets were protected from certain loss at the hands of thieves.

Nabal reaped the consequences for his lack of action. Even though David spared his life, God did not. Scripture records Nabal's judgment: "About ten days later, the Lord struck Nabal and he died" (1 Samuel 25:38).

Nabal was not the only one at fault, however. Look at David. He was behaving like an Old Testament *mafioso*. Nabal hadn't contracted with David for such protection. Nabal was not violating any agreement. Sure, it would have been nice for Nabal to voluntarily show some appreciation, but David was planning to commit cold-blooded murder of a man and his family simply because he didn't get invited to the sheep shearers' barbecue.

Remember, by this time, Saul had slain his thousands but David his ten thousands. In David's eyes, this stubborn man was no match for his troops. This is hardly the high point of David's life.

Abigail's allegiance to her husband is not the greatest example of how a loving marriage works either. She called her husband "fool" to another man. She took sides (not her husband's) and showed allegiance and loyalty to her husband's nemesis. (Wives, husbands are not generally encouraged by this.)

On the other hand, Abigail's security was threatened. She did what she had to do to protect her household and her husband's life. Abigail showed allegiance to righteousness and in so doing kept two egotistical and stubborn men from coming to blows. She addressed David because she knew her husband would not listen to reason. If she had wanted to be free from the man whose name means "fool," she could have simply stood by and done nothing and let David take him out. But her loyalty to her husband's continued existence motivated her to prevail on David's sense of justice.

While Abigail was certainly justified in acting to save the lives of her children, husband, and household—the *way* she talked to David provides a textbook example of how a woman gives a man her strong approval. Let's look closely at how she spoke to David. She knew the way to David's heart.

1. She assumed the best about David. She began with a *spoken* assumption that David wanted to live his life consistent with the will of God when she said, "Now

since the Lord has kept you, my master…" (verse 26). She powerfully communicated that she approved of him because the Lord approved of him.

2. She showed that she was willing to follow David's leading. By calling David "my master," she demonstrated she would willingly follow. Keep in mind that David was not yet the King of Israel. He was not legally her master. She was volunteering her allegiance even though she was not mandated to do so.

3. She spoke words of hope for David's future. She continued to demonstrate her loyalty by saying, "The Lord will certainly make a lasting dynasty for my master" (verse 28). Here she appealed to David's vision. God had told David that he was to become King of Israel. But for the moment, he was living in hiding and begging (and thinking of killing) for food.

4. She did not try to change David's life plan or vision. What if Abigail had tried to alter David's plans? She could have tempted David to save her life and do away with her foolish husband. She had a lot to offer: thousands of sheep and goats, land, houses, servants, "twelve-cylinder" camels—the works. Not to mention the best prize of all—herself. Abigail was beautiful and intelligent. A quick act of revenge and all of this would have been David's. But Abigail made no such offer. She did not tempt him to do something he would later regret. She encouraged him to pursue God's vision for his life with a clear conscience.

5. She told David that she found him to be a "good man." Abigail was just warming up. She gave more

strong words of approval when she said, "He fights the Lord's battle" (verse 28). Telling a man who seeks to serve God that "he fights the Lord's battle" is about the most positive reinforcement possible. David had to be feeling good about himself at this time.

6. She did not nag David but got him to change by a positive appeal. The brilliance of Abigail's discussion with David was how she delicately intertwined her approval and disapproval of his actions. After she built him up, she carefully moved to the heart of the issue. She did not criticize David for what he was about to do, but instead she helped him focus on the big picture. Abigail confronted David's momentary wrongdoing by saying, "Let no wrongdoing be found in you as long as you live" (verse 28). Notice she did not say, "What are you doing, you hothead? You come here threatening to kill my family. Who do you think we are? Goliath II? Going to bump off a man and his kids 'cause you didn't get invited to the barbecue? Just wait 'til *The Jerusalem Inquirer* hears about this one."

Abigail did not provoke him. Instead her words contained a built-in assumption that David normally did the right thing and that he wanted to obey God's standards. She simply appealed to him to live up to the lofty ideals that she believed were in David's heart. Abigail could have criticized David for all of his mistakes in the past and present. If she had, David probably would have said to himself, "I'll show her how bad I can be."

Abigail chose to set before David a high moral and godly standard for him to live up to. As she spoke she knew his heart intentions (not necessarily his actions) were to follow God's standard.

7. She showed that she knew and cared about David's troubles. She said, "Even though someone is pursuing you to take your life…" (verse 29). This let him know that she understood the anxiety that he was facing. She knew he didn't really want to do the wrong thing.

8. She spoke positive words for his future. She encouraged him with beautiful words of hope for the future when she said, "The life of my master will be bound securely in the bundle of the living by the Lord your God" (verse 29). Abigail inspired David to pursue a higher standard. She showed him light at the end of his dark tunnel.

As a result, David replied to her, "May you be blessed for your good judgment and for keeping me from bloodshed this day and from avenging myself with my own hands" (verse 31). David was so inspired by Abigail's wisdom and allegiance that after Nabal died, he immediately asked Abigail to be his wife.

Wisdom can be gained from Abigail's approach. In spite of the fact that David was not her husband, Abigail knew how to communicate respect and loyalty. She knew how to diffuse a tense situation and inspire a willing man to pursue godliness.

Do you inspire your husband or discourage him by your words? Do you motivate him to live up to your high expectations of him or do you criticize him to the point of making him feel worse about himself? People have a tendency to live up or down to what others think of them.

Are your conversations with your husband laced with assumptions that you know he wants to do the will of God? You communicate your approval of your husband every time you say something that reflects a positive assumption about his character. When you speak to him or about him, your words tell your husband that you believe in him 100 percent and that you respect him for who he is. If, on the other hand, you communicate an underlying assumption that you think your husband normally wants to function outside of God's will, you communicate disapproval that strikes at his core. Any time you say, "There you go again," or words to that effect, you have shown disapproval that chips away at your husband's heart.

Do you demonstrate that you are willing to follow your husband's leadership? Do you take his side in the battles of life even when he may not be doing it the way you think he should? When you need to confront him with a mistake, do you follow Abigail's example with David by communicating your belief that this is a momentary glitch from a man who you normally find to be "right on"? Do you take the time to understand your husband's needs, troubles, and circumstances? No matter what kind of job your husband has, he has troubles. And unless he is a CIA agent and is forbidden to tell you about work, you should take the initiative to find out about the "Sauls" in his life who are pursuing him.

Finally, do you show your abiding approval and loyalty by talking warmly about your husband's future, making it clear that you want to be a central part of it?

One of the most powerful means of communicating approval is to willingly attach yourself to your husband's future by speaking words of hope. Do you try to give your husband encouragement to continue on with God's will for his life? Or do you try to repaint your husband's vision with your own set of watercolors? He should have the wisdom to use you as a sounding board and partner in determining his dreams in the first place, but once they are there, you should be a constant source of loyal encouragement, rather than giving in to the natural temptation to remake your husband in your own image.

If you practice telling your husband his strengths rather than pointing out his faults, your husband is going to be more than a happy camper—he will be thrilled. If you don't practice these "Abigail skills," the sad reality is there are always one or more Abigails out there who will. A husband who feels continuously criticized by his wife often gives in to temptation when a more uplifting person comes along.

While your husband will probably remain true in his actions, his heart and mind may wander if your actions leave him feeling unsupported and unloved. Remember David's reaction. He was very attracted to Abigail. He asked her to marry him at his first opportunity.

Hindrances to Giving Approval and Allegiance

Being as loyal as Ruth and as inspiring as Abigail may seem like a tough order. If you have been practicing disloyalty and discouragement for a decade or more, how do you switch gears? Over the years you and your husband may have learned how to skillfully manipulate each other. You may be afraid to change the way in which you speak to each other. You are comfortable with your dissatisfying relationship. If you desire to change your ways, consider some of the hindrances that may keep you from giving your husband your approval and allegiance.

1. Failing to verbalize your approval

Although men are reputed to be "non-verbal," most women could also improve their natural verbal abilities by expressing more words of approval and allegiance to their husbands. It is not enough to think warm thoughts about your husband. It is imperative to regularly, even frequently, verbalize your approval and allegiance to him.

When I (Mike) am traveling, I find that my wife and I have some of our best conversations over the phone. We take a little extra time with each other that we might not take if we were together face-to-face with the whirl of activity that defines the Farris household. Our long-distance conversations often give me the "attaboys" that every man so desperately desires.

It is impossible to overstate the importance of verbalizing your approval of your husband. Many men are unfaithful to their wives, not because the "other woman" is more physically attractive or simply for theoretically more exciting sexual escapades, but rather because they find great attraction to women who build them up. Men, like women, want to be wanted. They want to be approved. If a man's wife is a constant source of complaints and disapproval, the husband will face greater temptation to go elsewhere where he can find an encouraging word. Husbands are never justified in God's eyes when they wander. But if a man feels put down by his wife far more often than he feels built up, then he will feel self-justified if he is tempted to seek love somewhere else. Although self-justification is sinful and delusional, it is the sad reality for many men.

Remember Christ's example:

> Do not judge, and you will not be judged. Do not condemn, and you will not be condemned. Forgive, and you will be forgiven. Give and it will be given to you. A good measure, pressed down, shaken together and running over, will be poured into your lap. For with the measure you use, it will be measured to you. (Luke 6:37-38)

The more you are critical of your husband, the more he will be critical of you. The opposite is also true. The more you praise him and give him your approval, the more he will give praise and approval back. Change your negative communication habits, and you will change your husband. He will desire to live up to your positive beliefs about him. Give him more positive feedback than you feel capable of, and he will start to deserve more and more of your praise.

2. Waiting for perfection

Your husband is no Prince Charming. My wife knows that I certainly am not. No man is perfect nor even close to this mark. But knowing this does not necessarily prevent a wife from wistfully dreaming of "the ideal husband." Don't forget, however, it is just as wrong to fall in love with a fictitious dream of perfection as it is to fall in love with another man. If you fail to love your husband fully because you are wistfully wanting Mr. Ideal to come sweeping into your life, you are engaging in emotional adultery.

Jesus made it clear that all forms of adultery are sin. There are different (and normally lesser) consequences for emotional adultery than for physical adultery, but the consequences are still substantial and the sin is still grievous in the sight of God. God accepts us as we are; yet He also expects us to meet His standards.

Be careful of where you get your ideas of what your husband should be like. Romance novels with their perfect gentlemen can create ideals in your mind that are more fantasy than reality. Magazine articles can also influence your expectations. We have all seen, while waiting to check out at the grocery store, magazine articles about "Ten Things Every Woman Wants from Her Man." Women begin comparing their husbands to the ten things on the list and soon discover that their husbands are severely lacking in a number of areas. Women can create standards for their husbands that are unreasonable and unreachable. Expectations should line up with God's expectations. If they do not, then someone has to adjust (it will not be God).

Be loyal to your husband in your emotions and dreams. If you find yourself dreaming of how your husband can be a little bit better, that's O.K. But keep your hopes and your heart focused on him. Dwell on his positive traits rather than his negative traits when you think of him throughout the day.

3. Withholding forgiveness and becoming bitter

Unforgiveness is a major roadblock that hinders you from giving your husband approval. The longer you hold his mistakes against him, the more bitter you become. Your husband may have made a poor decision or handled something wrong in the past. If you have forgiven him and moved on, then your hurt is only a memory. If you have not forgiven him for a past mistake, then day by day your hurt toward your husband will increase. Every time he does something wrong you will add his offense to the last unforgiven offense. Instead of feeling hurt over one offense, now you have added yet another and then another. The list will continue to grow until you learn to forgive. Your resentment will become so great that you will lose any feeling of love that you once had for him.

Unforgiveness over time can build up like the layers of grease on your range hood. Small hurts and disappointments add layer upon layer. Each layer isn't much to see; yet after awhile they build up until they can't be ignored.

Marriage without forgiveness is like a flower without rain. Just as a flower must have water to survive, so must a marriage have the cleansing power of forgiveness. When we forgive, God is able to take the hurt and replace it with peace. If we do not forgive, it is like we are shackled to a ball and chain. Everywhere we go, we pull the extra weight with us. Our thoughts, emotions, and our spirit are burdened by our inability to forgive.

When we forgive, we take the hurt and leave it at Christ's feet. We may not forget the event (we can't erase history), but we can release it to Christ and move on. If there are events or memories that you continue to struggle with, you might be harboring unforgiveness. If unforgiveness is not dealt with, it can develop into bitterness.

Hebrews 12:15 warns against the danger of bitterness: "See to it that no one misses the grace of God and that no bitter root grows up to cause trouble and defile many." Bitterness usually begins in an area of our lives where we have been hurt once or repeatedly. The problem with bitterness is that it does not stay confined to one area. It grows and spreads into other areas of our lives.

One summer in the corner of our yard near the back fence, some poison ivy began to grow. I (Reed) didn't want our children to get in it, so I decided I would keep it cut down when I mowed the yard. After a few weeks I found the poison ivy was beginning to grow up on my neighbor's side of my fence. Since the fence was on my property, I decided I would mow the poison ivy down on that side of the fence also. After a few more weeks of this, I discovered that the poison ivy was growing up on the other side of the fence corner, in another neighbor's yard. I finally wised up and realized I couldn't keep mowing everyone else's yard. I would have to get rid of it some other way.

Poison ivy was not a problem that could be dealt with on the surface. It was a root problem. Poison ivy has an extensive root network. It goes down under the ground and spreads out, so it can grow up in many directions. If you want to rid yourself of it, you must dig up all the roots, not just cut off the visible growth on the surface.

Poison ivy is a good example of how bitterness works. It begins with some unforgiveness but doesn't stay contained there. The bitterness spreads into how you begin to see others, how you see yourself, how you interpret life. We have all seen bitter people. We work with them, go to church with them, are related to them, but we politely call them pessimists. They really are bitter people. What they say and think springs from a bitter root.

Your husband may have hurt you in a major way or in small ways over and over again. Now you are resistant or hesitant to give him your allegiance or approval. Examine you heart for unforgiveness or bitterness. Then pray about what God would have you do. Don't allow the roots of bitterness to grow in your heart. The longer you allow bitterness to grow, the harder it is to get rid of. Remember the best way to forgive is…often.

4. Remaking your husband in your image

There is nothing wrong with encouraging your husband to do right. In the area of God's moral law, there is only one standard of behavior—obedience to God. Gently encourage your husband (remember Abigail's style) to obey God's moral law if he is ever tempted to cut corners.

But there are so many areas of life where the decisions do not involve God's moral law, but rather involve individual leading and direction from the Lord. Most career choices, for example, fall into this category.

Your husband should have a vision for his life and some general life goals that he is pursuing. You can and should reinforce the vision that God has given your husband, but you shouldn't be doing the leading. Your husband should consult with you to help establish or update his goals, but understand the difference between giving your husband some feedback as opposed to manipulating him to get him to do what you want. Do not force him to fit into the mold that you desire for him, but desire God's mold for his life.

The best way to inspire your husband to reach his goals is to let him know that you believe in his ability to accomplish them. Some women try to push their husbands to reach their goals through nagging. This type of pushing usually results in resistance. Instead of pushing, consider praying. The best "pushing" is done on your knees.

You can gently state your concerns or opinions to your husband, but once he has heard you, resist the temptation to "nag" him about the matter. Instead, take your concerns to God in prayer. Tell God over and over again. He will listen. Unlike your husband, He doesn't mind being nagged. Remember the parable of the widow who continued to bother the judge (Luke 18)? She continued knocking on his door until he answered her request for justice against her adversary. Jesus encouraged us not to give up praying when He said, "And will not God bring about justice for His chosen ones, who cry out to Him day and night? Will He keep putting them off?" (Luke 18:7). Jesus is the One who can speak directly to your husband's heart. Take your concerns to Him, and He will answer you.

The Rewards of Loyalty

Your prayers will free God's hand to do the work that only He can do in your marriage. Showing your husband that you approve of him often will make him feel loved and accepted by you. When his need for approval is met, he will not need to look for it in other relationships. Being loyal to your husband in the easy times and the difficult times will increase his confidence to lead. Your marriage relationship will be greatly strengthened when you begin to show your husband loyalty. Your chances of you and your husband fulfilling your vow "till death do us part" will be remarkably increased. Accept the challenge today to become your husband's strongest advocate.

Let your gentleness be evident to all. The Lord is at hand.

Philippians 4:5

Husbands, in the same way be considerate as you live with your wives.

1 Peter 3:7a

3

A WIFE NEEDS HER HUSBAND'S
Gentleness and Compassion

Attributes of Gentleness and Compassion
- A husband needs to be physically gentle
- A husband needs to be emotionally gentle
- A husband needs to show Christlike compassion

Physical Gentleness

*S*ome basic attributes of gentleness are non-negotiable. A husband should be physically and emotionally respectful of his beloved. Physical gentleness begins with the absolute rule that there is no place whatsoever for hitting one's wife or threatening to do so. It should go without saying that violence toward your mate is the antithesis of gentleness. Hurting your wife in any way is completely contrary to the principle of "loving your wife as Christ loved the Church and gave Himself up for her" (Ephesians 5:25).

If you struggle in this area, you need to seek help from a pastor or a Christian counselor. You owe it to your wife to get your anger under control. She will never trust you completely until you are able to control yourself. If you are physically harming your wife, you are also breaking the law and you could end up in jail. Get help immediately.

Maybe violence is not a problem for you. You would never consider hitting your wife. But, like many men, you may struggle with respecting your wife's body when it comes to sex. The simple rule is this: Do not engage in any sexual behavior that hurts or harms your wife. Similarly, do not force your wife to engage in any sexual activity that she finds distasteful or unacceptable.

A healthy physical relationship between a man and a wife is built on respect and trust. Your wife should feel that you always have her best interest at heart. If sex is forced or expected whenever you want it, sex will become a duty rather than a pleasure for her.

Your touch should communicate to your wife that you value her like a priceless jewel. Let your touch tell her you love her. She wants to be kissed now and then for the simple pleasure of kissing. Kissing should not have to always lead to more involved sexual activity.

Your wife desires romance throughout the day, not just in the bedroom. Holding her hand, touching her cheek, rubbing her shoulders gives her the affection she desires outside the context of sex.

Men have a strong and powerful desire for sex. While women also have a desire for sex, it is secondary to their desire for love and companionship that can best be described as emotional oneness. Sexual activity that proceeds without first having established emotional unity is rarely pleasing or truly acceptable to a wife. This is one of the most frequent ways that sex is misused within marriage.

Today's culture is focused on pleasing self at all costs. This fixation has even crept into the church. Many Christian husbands lack self-control when it comes to sex. Men, if we are to be leaders in our homes, we must be examples of self-control. The world says, "Indulge yourself—you deserve it." The Bible says, "Die to self—put others before yourself" (Galatians 2:20). This includes honoring your wife sexually.

People have died from a lack of food, water, oxygen, and even shelter; but no one has died because of a lack of sex. Jesus fasted from food for forty days, and He grew stronger. Husbands, are we men enough to control our bodies in the sexual area?

Achieving Emotional Oneness

Self-control, in the interest of your wife, is the duty of a loving husband. But we think you will discover that if you follow our advice about achieving emotional oneness, you will find that your wife will be more willing and more excited about your sexual relationship. Make sure that before you begin to engage in the physical side of your relationship with your wife that you have taken the temperature of your emotional relationship. Take some time to listen to your wife and to respond to her needs for emotional oneness. Keep in mind, however, that listening is far more important than responding. It is also appropriate to spend some time sharing what is going on in your inner-person as well. Your wife is looking for emotional oneness before she will desire physical oneness.

One of the reasons that Vickie and I (Mike) have such a strong marriage after nearly thirty years is that we have made it our consistent practice to be at peace with each other before we engage in a physical relationship. Even if we have to stay up until three or four in the morning (which we have to do once or twice a year), we are absolutely committed to working things out.

One couple I (Reed) counseled was having problems with their sex life. The problem was it had no life! As we worked together, I discovered they were in a cycle of unmet needs. The wife felt unfulfilled emotionally and found it difficult to give of herself sexually. The husband felt unfulfilled sexually and found it difficult to give emotionally. To break this cycle, the husband began focusing on emotional oneness rather than physical oneness with his wife. As he began meeting his wife's emotional needs, his wife was drawn closer to him, and her passion for him was rekindled. She was then more receptive to his sexual advances.

When a married couple makes emotional oneness their focus, physical oneness will follow closely behind.

Emotional closeness will increase the couple's desire to be physically close.

Husbands, if you want to both honor your wife *and* improve your sex life, make emotional oneness your first priority.

Emotional Gentleness

For every opportunity we have to demonstrate physical gentleness, we will have multiple opportunities to shower our wives with emotional gentleness. I (Mike) cringe every time I hear a man make a joke about his wife. With rare exceptions, these jokes are simply belittling words that tear at the wife's insides. These kinds of "jokes" are inappropriate outside of the presence of one's wife. And they are doubly inappropriate in her presence. I love to tell jokes and consider my ability to make off-the-cuff humorous comments to be above average. But I follow a strict rule that I will never make a "humorous" comment about my wife, without her explicit advance permission.

For example, in one of my regular home schooling talks I mention, as I do in this book, that Vickie can write a $300 grocery list on one Post-It note. As innocent as that comment may seem, I make it with Vickie's permission. She, too, views it as innocent humor that simply describes her penmanship and in no way puts her down.

But many put-downs are not even arguably jokes. They are just gruff statements designed to make one's wife feel inferior. While some men think such statements make them "the big man," I personally think only a big idiot stoops to the point in life where he thinks that degrading his wife somehow upgrades his own standing. Sarcasm is the first cousin of the put-down. Don't give in to the temptation to be sarcastic to your wife or about your wife.

Both spouses would do well to follow the rules of "no put-downs in public" and "no put-downs in private." Today, "put-downs" are a popular style of humor. They are nothing more than insults behind a thin veil of humor. This style of humor can be destructive to your marriage. Proverbs points out the jagged edge of sarcasm: "Like a madman shooting firebrands or deadly arrows is a man who deceives his neighbor and says, 'I was only joking!'" (Proverbs 26:18-19).

We are to build up and edify each other. Why tear down your spouse? "Like a city whose walls are broken down is a man who lacks self-control" (Proverbs 25:28). If you need to talk to each other about a negative situation, get alone and do it with gentleness. And remember the presence of your children makes a situation public. Their little ears should never hear Dad put down Mom (or vice versa).

Christians have a sophisticated version of the "put-down" called the "prayer request." Prayer requests that belittle a spouse or dwell on their faults are still put-downs. Vickie has a special friend with whom she shares more details of her life than anyone else except me. She often shares prayer requests with her friend; but because of my respect and trust for this woman's confidentiality,

I am content with the fact that Vickie will sometimes share things with her, even about me, that I would not want shared elsewhere. I have a similar friendship with another man in our church. But even in these relationships, we have clearly implied limits beyond which we will not go.

A commitment to emotional gentleness means that you respect the privacy of your marriage and the intimate secrets of your wife's heart. When she shares her hopes, dreams, fears, and concerns with you, you should not break confidence by telling someone else.

Christlike Compassion

Men seek passion far more often than they demonstrate compassion. (Read that sentence about three times to make sure you get it.) Compassion for your wife means that you seek to infuse your wife's daily life with understanding and a loving spirit.

A home schooling mom needs a lot of understanding. Because of the daily activity needed to complete academic instruction, a home schooling mom is very pressed to get to all the housework, cleaning, and cooking that she would otherwise like to get done. When a compassionate husband arrives home from work, he sizes up the situation at home and helps where needed. A husband who walks in and says, "I see dinner's going to be late again" has just failed the compassion test.

Try an experiment. Take a day off work and watch what your wife does. Better yet, try to do what your wife does for one day without her help. Cook, clean, wash clothes, discipline, teach, and chauffeur five kids all over town and see how your nerves are at the end of the day. I guarantee you that you will be quite anxious for your wife to come home and encourage you and help you get through the rest of the day.

A few years ago while sitting in an elders' meeting discussing some of the difficulties of satisfying the needs of our growing congregation, I (Mike) began to feel a great deal of empathy and compassion for our pastor. At the time, he was the only staff person (he did not even have a part-time secretary) for a congregation of about 180 people. All the elders in our church are extraordinarily busy. We help with church matters whenever we can to shoulder the burden of problems that are inherent in any church. But all the elders, except the pastor, have jobs outside of the church and activities that dominate our lives on a regular basis. We are never saddled with the responsibility that a pastor has. He has no mental escape. This is his job, his church, and his life in a much more significant way than for us as volunteer elders. Mental escape is a rare and difficult occurrence. Being a pastor is tough.

Just as a pastor has a difficult time obtaining a mental escape from his round-the-clock job, our wives also have a version of round-the-clock responsibilities as home schooling moms and wives.

I try my best to spoil my wife. Very often I call home in the late afternoon a half-hour or so before she would begin preparations for dinner. I check up on her and try to gauge her emotional and physical stamina. I ask about the plans for the evening and specifically her plans for dinner. If it appears to me that her stamina in either category is running too low, I will often offer to bring home pizza or hamburgers or else go to the store to get something that is simple enough for me to cook for dinner.

Other than dinner (cooking it and cleaning it up), the second most stressful event of the evening for most home schooling moms is putting the kids to bed. I must confess that it is easier for me to pitch in and help with dinner than it is for me to help with bedtime. Often I have become engaged in some project (some worthwhile, some purely frivolous) and I simply don't want to tear myself away. Even as I write this, I am convicted that I need to be more compassionate toward my wife concerning the bedtime routine with our children. She desires my help, but more than that she desires my compassionate understanding of all the difficulties that she faces all day. Women can see quite clearly into the hearts of their husbands, at least in terms of assessing their motives. They need our understanding love every bit as much as they need our actual help.

Another way to demonstrate our compassion is to infuse our wives' daily lives with a spirit of love. The old-fashioned and very appropriate way to begin this process is to simply tell your wife that you love her as often as you possibly can. The soft touches of flowers, small gifts, and thoughtful notes will undoubtedly win the heart of your wife anew.

These acts of compassion communicate a powerful message to your wife. They tell her that in the midst of your own busyness, you have taken the time to really consider her life, understand her, and take actions that show she occupies a place of real value in your heart. Every woman needs to know that her husband feels that way about her. And virtually no wife can resist a man who treats her with this kind of creative, practical compassion.

How beautiful you are, my darling! Oh, how beautiful!

Song of Solomon 4:1

4

A HUSBAND NEEDS HIS WIFE'S

Affection and Beauty

Attributes of Affection and Beauty
- A wife needs to recognize that men and women are different
- A wife needs to resist a "Don't touch me!" attitude
- A wife should remember that a good sex life involves spiritual warfare
- A wife should realize she is a role model for her children

I (Reed) often share a joke with clients who are having sexual difficulties to help give some perspective to their problem: Do you know why God did not give women the same sex drive as men? Because if He did, we would never get anything else done in life.

Men and women do have different desires for affection and sex. Men's sex drives have been compared to microwaves, whereas women's sex drives are more like crock-pots. Men (in general) are ready for sex anytime. Women, on the other hand, take a while to heat up. Like a crock-pot, you turn it on in the morning, add some ingredients throughout the day, and by dinnertime the meal is ready.

Men and Women Are Different

Men and women have different emotional capacities that affect their sex drives. Men have the ability to have a bad day at the office, come home to a hectic home school day, fix a home-repair crisis, feel exhausted, and yet still be "in the mood" when they go to bed. The old cliché that men have "one-track minds" is true. They set out to pursue a goal, accomplish that goal, and then move on. Men are simple (and I did not say simple-minded, ladies!). They have an ability to keep things separated.

Women are more complex. They are like radar sweeping across the homefront taking in everything. I (Reed) can come home and find my wife making supper while talking on the phone. At the same time she can hear a noise upstairs, recognize that a certain child is into something he shouldn't be into, and direct me to which room in the house. She is multi-functional. She can do several tasks at once. If you put me in the same scenario, I would burn dinner while I talked on the phone as the children tore up the house. Or I could make dinner, ignore and offend whoever is on the phone, and forget the children are left alone. Or I could watch the children, burn dinner, and offend whoever is on the phone. You get the idea. I'm simple—one thing at a time, please.

Emotional Differences

How do emotional differences between men and women affect their sex lives? Men have a greater ability to keep everything separate in their minds that happened throughout the day. Women's thoughts are more intermingled. Everything that happens throughout the day is interconnected—it all flows together. A husband can have a terrible day at the office, yet when it's time for bed, he can refocus his mind on sex. Ladies, you may be amazed that he can be "frisky" after all that has happened. Just remember, you and your husbands are different in the sexual desire department. He has separated everything. The other happenings of the day are all put into their compartments, and now only one thing is on his mind. Just as he is trying to "live with his wife in an understanding way" (1 Peter 3:7), you can also try to live with him in an understanding way.

For men sex is like breathing. A study once found that the average male thought of sex several times per day. We all have different needs in different areas. Some people need eight to ten hours of sleep a night, while others need six to eight hours. Some people eat a little food; others need a lot to keep their bodies running.

The frequency of a couple's lovemaking will vary according to their age and individual sex drives.

Depending on their lifestyle and what stage of life they are in usually determines whether they have sex once a day or once every couple of months. The most demanding stage of marriage is the child-rearing stage. As home schoolers we have to keep in mind that the level of stress in our lives will impact our sex lives.

Physical Differences

In general, a man's sex drive peaks in intensity around the age of eighteen. He may maintain this level of need through his mid-twenties. At this time he may desire intercourse from five to seven times a week. A gradual decline over the years ensues. As long as a man maintains his physical and emotional health, he may remain sexually active into his eighties and beyond. In the later years it may take longer to achieve erection and ejaculation. Parts may move slower, but they still work.

A woman usually reaches the peak of her sex drive in her late twenties to early thirties. At this peak she may desire intercourse much less than men at their peak. She, however, does not experience a decrease in desire over the years. In a woman's later years, she may match and even exceed her mate's desire for sex. With the changes in sexual expression in our culture, it is not uncommon for women to express themselves and their desires more openly to their husbands.

When you read the Song of Solomon in the Bible, you notice a difference in perspective between the two genders. The male point of view is visually-oriented. He talks about her appearance. He describes her eyes like those of a dove's, her lips like a strand of scarlet, her neck like the tower of David, her breasts like two fawns, and the curves of her thighs like jewels. When is the last time you and your husband talked about your "gazelles"? The Shulamite woman speaks from a different point of view. She talks of his presence, his scent, and his reputation at the city gate. Their perspectives vary greatly.

Ladies, you may get tired of your husband looking at you every time you undress. It is a natural thing for men to do—they are visual. You do not need to be upset if he is looking at you. In my experience as a counselor, I have found that you may need to worry if he is not looking at you when you undress.

Don't Buy the Lie!

One of the major television networks has a segment on its evening news called "The Fleecing of America." It is a segment that exposes how Americans are being taken advantage of. It reminds me (Reed) of what I call "The Over-Sexing of America." We live in a sexual age. Sex is one of the major focuses of our society. The permissive, sexual ideas of the sixties have become the standard today, even though they have been proven to be harmful to relationships, marriage, and sex. "Free love" isn't really free—it has many strings attached.

The culture has tainted our perspective of sex. No longer is old-fashioned, normal sex adequate to fulfill sexual desires. Now couples tend to "need" to experience kinky sex to keep their marriage fresh, exciting, and romantic.

Bizarre sex can seem exciting all right, but that is a road that can develop an appetite that gets out of control. I work with people who are at times overcoming addictions. None of them would say that they started out with the intention of getting addicted. It was at first just "fun."

The same addictive cycle can happen in our sex lives. What begins as "fun" becomes a habit, an urge that has to be fed more and more to be satisfied. A couple may simply experiment with some kinky lingerie, then some "how to" books, and then some videos, and the slippery slope heads further down to the pit.

When humans were created, "the man and his wife were both naked, and they felt no shame" (Genesis 2:25). Make your spouse the pure object of your passion and keep the ways of our culture out of your bedroom.

One husband I counseled had been addicted to pornography before he was married, and he struggled with his addiction off and on during his marriage. His ideas about what sex was supposed to be and his wife's ideas were very different. He was always pushing for something new and different. It began to make her feel like she was inadequate. In one session she voiced that she felt when it came time for sex, she always had to put on a performance. Eventually, she began to resent the pressure he was putting on her. This is not the way God designed sex to work.

In 1 Corinthians 6:19, the Bible clearly explains how we should respect our bodies: "Do you not know that your body is a temple of the Holy Spirit, who is in you, whom you have received from God?" Since our bodies are the temples of the Holy Spirit, nothing should be done that will physically or emotionally harm our spouses or ourselves. Also nothing should be done that will degrade either spouse. Common Christian courtesy says that each spouse is a child of God and should be respected. Nothing should be done coercively, but by mutual desire and consent.

Don't Touch Me!

Home schooling mothers who have several smaller children may become "touched-out." Throughout the day a mother has children sitting on her lap, holding her hand, hugging her neck, grabbing her knees, and maybe even a baby nursing at her breast. All of the touching she receives can fulfill her need for physical contact. By the time her husband comes home, she is not necessarily hungering for hugs and kisses. She is more likely thinking, "Don't touch me!" Her husband, on the other hand, in the workplace receives no more than an occasional handshake. His need for physical contact is not met. Wives need to be sensitive to their husbands' need for a hug and a kiss when he comes home.

A German group of psychologists, physicians, and insurance companies cooperated on a research project designed to find the secret to long life and success. They made a surprising discovery. The secret? Kiss your wife each morning when you leave for work! The meticulous German researchers discovered that men who kiss their wives every morning have fewer automobile accidents on their way to work than men who omit the morning kiss. The good-morning kissers also miss less work because of illness and earn 20 to 30 percent more money than non-kissers. How do they explain their findings? According to West Germany's Dr. Arthur Szabo, "A husband who kisses his wife every morning begins the day with a positive attitude."[1] How would your husband's attitude change in your home for the evening if you greeted your spouse when he got home with a hug and a kiss? Over time there would probably be some tangible results.

What stage of life we are in greatly influences our desire for intimacy and at times our opportunity. As a home schooling father of six, I (Reed) have to chuckle about people's assumptions and comments about our sex life. Since we have six children, they assume we must have a very active sex life. They are right about one thing—our life is very active. In reality, when you have six children, having a sex life gets challenging with all the demands on your time. My wife has a recurring dream (or nightmare) that every time we are trying to have some time of intimacy someone is knocking on the bedroom door.

Too Little Time

I have found that home schoolers have some unique factors that affect their sexual relationship. One of them that affects the wife is the increased demands on her. Not only is she now wife, mother, housekeeper, chauffeur, cook, and chief bottle washer, but now she is also the teacher! At times she is going to be greatly fatigued or just plain exhausted at the end of the day. What is different between your home schooling wife and other mothers is that she can't leave her stress or demands at the office (if she works outside the home) because she is at her office. She also doesn't get the uninterrupted hours while children are at school to complete her daily tasks. She has to juggle everybody and everything in the same place (home). One home schooling mother remarked, "Everybody needs you for this or that all day long. At the end of the day there is your husband in line too, waiting for sex."

Time can become a factor that hinders a good sex life. There never seems to be enough time in the day for everything we want to accomplish. "Too-ness" is also a major factor. We are too tired, too low on energy, too busy, too stressed, or too preoccupied. Other times we are just not in the mood, or we have false expectations of what a normal sex life really is. The way around all of this is simply saving enough of yourself in reserve to give to your husband. Jesus spent his life giving to others. He is our example. I see couples who pour themselves into raising their children, home schooling their children, and doing their best for their children; yet they have nothing left to give to their marriages. A good marriage is the foundation of a good home for your children.

As challenging as it may seem, ladies, you dare not live your life in a way which expends all of your energy so as to leave your husband out day after day. Pace yourself better. Cut some things out if you have to. Find a curriculum that may not be as ideal as you would like if the change gives you more time and energy. Stop being a home school support group leader. Do something—*if* you regularly are rebuffing your husband's desire for sex due to exhaustion. Obviously, this would also be an ideal time to point out to your husband how it would serve everyone's interests if he helped more in the evening. But, ultimately, something has to change so that you have adequate time for each other.

This is not just our opinion. The Bible gives the answer in very clear terms. "Do not deprive each other except by mutual consent and for a time, so that you may devote yourselves to prayer. Then come together again so that Satan will not tempt you because of your lack of self-control" (1 Corinthians 7:5).

Talk About It!

Talk with your spouse about what pleases you sexually. Tell him your likes and dislikes, what feels good, what doesn't. Communication is essential if you want your sexual relationship to be good for both of you. Unspoken desires can become a source of contention between you because you won't know how to please each other.

How you were instructed about sex by your parents influences how you communicate about sex to your spouse. Many parents just hand their adolescent a book about sex and hope that somehow the child will make sense of it all. When I (Reed) was in junior high school my parents gave me a booklet on venereal disease. I didn't quite understand how someone actually contracted the disease, but after reading the book, I was convinced that I never wanted to catch it. As much as I can remember, a follow-up discussion with my parents about sex never happened. Sex was just one of those subjects that was "off-limits."

We need to get past whatever taboos we were raised with when it comes to talking about sex. Sex is not dirty, shameful, or wrong. God invented sex. The Bible says He wants to give us good things—sex included.

A Good Sex Life Is Spiritual Warfare

A man's sex drive is a strong force within him. He may seem to be an animal at times, pawing you and grabbing you to let you know "I need sex." This sex drive is a powerful force. It can change a normal, intelligent, moral man into a misguided fool. This drive causes upstanding businessmen, politicians, church leaders, and others to throw away their reputations, careers and marriages for a sexual relationship. It is as if their minds turn to mush. This is not an excuse for adultery. Not every man gives into his flesh. Many men stick to their convictions about marriage, but unfortunately not every man does.

Some women make the mistake of living in denial about their husbands' sexual vulnerability. They naively think, "My husband would never have an affair. He wouldn't do that to me." We all hope that. Yet there are no guarantees. Avoiding denial sounds like this, "I know my husband likes sex, and I do not want him to be tempted to have an affair. What can I do to help prevent the situation?"

When you have a realistic perspective of your husband's vulnerability, you can take measures to make him strong where he is weak. The best weapon against adultery is for a husband and wife to develop a good sex life together. A minister once summed it up this way, "Why should your husband look at hamburgers when he has steak waiting for him at home?" Temptation is always waiting for you, but can only have power over you if you walk outside the walls of God's protection. When you learn how to enjoy your spouse, the temptation to have sexual relationships outside of marriage will be much easier to resist. The enemy won't have a chance. Wives, you can help your husband resist temptation by becoming irresistible in his eyes. He won't want anyone else when he knows that you want him.

Respect Your Differences

Very early in marriage, a husband and wife usually discover how different they are. Janine and I quickly realized that we had different requirements for sleep. We had to learn how to adjust our sleeping habits so that both of our needs were met. I do not make her get up when I do, and she does not make me come to bed when she does. Friction happens in marriage when we find ourselves at different points, and no one is willing to change.

When it comes to our desire for sex, sometimes we are both in the mood, and sometimes only one of us is in the mood. When only one of us desires sex, we try to practice the principle found in Romans 12:10: "Honor one another above yourselves." When we strive to please each other above ourselves, we honor each other. This is especially important when it comes to sex. For instance, a husband in the mood may say to his tired wife, "I understand this is a bad time for you. You have had a long, stressful day. I can wait till a better time." Or, a wife may say, "Even though I've had a long day, I desire to be with you."

This is the peaceable way that God designed sex in marriage to work, a man and wife honoring each other's needs. When a husband or wife is self-centered, only desiring to fulfill his or her sexual needs, sooner or later sexual tension will develop between the couple.

Beauty Is in the Eye of the Beholder

What originally attracted your husband to you? It may have been your brains, your personality, or spiritual maturity, but your appearance was certainly an attraction too. When you first met, you both paid attention to every detail. You were concerned about how you looked, what the plans were for the evening, what you would eat, and where you would go.

Many women continue to pay attention to their appearance after they are married, but for some beauty becomes a memory of their youth. Once children come along, they let their appearance slide. To save time in the morning, they begin throwing on a pair of sweats, forgoing the make-up, and diving in to the activities of the day.

Some say women are guilty of false advertising. When they are dating their husbands, they present themselves as attentive to their appearance, but after marriage their appearance becomes a low priority. Keeping the house beautiful and their kids dressed well becomes more important.

Keep in mind that men are visually stimulated. Just remember this joke: "Do you know why most women are more concerned with their beauty than their brains? Because most men see better than they think." Get the point? Men are attracted to beauty. Your attention to your appearance may well have been one of the things that attracted him to you in the beginning. He values your appearance, so you should too.

Looking beautiful does not require you to look like a woman on the cover of *Vogue* magazine. That cover girl is not real. (A graphic artist has touched up what the plastic surgeons missed!) Being beautiful for your husband requires being attentive to his visual needs. Find out what's important to him. Maybe he prefers your hair a certain way or maybe he likes it when you wear a certain perfume. Ask him to be honest with you about your clothes. Are they attractive to him?

Having children changes a woman's body in many ways. The goal is not to look like you did at eighteen, but to be as beautiful as you can be at forty or fifty or whatever your age may be. Physical changes that are a natural consequence of aging or childbearing are out of your control, but you can spiff up what you have to work with.

It is also important to remember that when your husband first fell in love with you, he fell in love with all of you—your brains, your looks, and your personality. Your appearance is only one aspect of the picture he sees when he looks at you. If you look great on the outside, but ugly words flow from your mouth when you speak to him, your attention to your appearance will not help much. Become a beautiful person inside and out. Let your outward and your inward appearance be pleasing to your husband.

Maybe you are thinking right now, "My husband should love me just as I am." That is true. He should love you because he said, "I do till death do us part." But, keeping up your appearance is just one more way for you to say, "I love you. I value you, and I want to please you with my appearance." Valuing your appearance is a way of honoring him. It is an absolute certainty that your husband will appreciate it if you do what you can to look your best.

You Are a Role Model

It is not only important to keep up your appearance for your husband but also for your children. "What!" you say. "My children? They love me like I am. I'm Mom—the one who is always there for them. They don't care what I look like." They may not care, but they are modeling you. You are their example of what a wife and mother is. Consciously or unconsciously, your daughters will try to emulate you. Your sons will compare whomever they marry to your example. It is not just how great you cook, how clean the house is, or how nurturing you are, but also what you looked like while doing it. I am not saying you need to wear a formal gown with your hair done up while cleaning the house, but you can get up each day and put on an outfit that is suitable to wear in public.

You only look at your appearance a few times a day in the mirror, but your husband and children look at you all day long.

Ladies, the way you look may actually affect your daughter's future in a way you wouldn't suspect. When I (Mike) was in my teens my mom casually remarked that if you want to see what a girl is going to look like in her forties or fifties—take a look at her mother. I seized on that remark like a hot stock tip and remembered it in the years that followed.

Beautiful Rewards

Giving some attention to your appearance can also affect your mood. I (Reed) worked with a client who was severely depressed. She got up in the morning and either stayed in her pajamas, or put on a sweat suit, and dragged herself through her daily routine. At some point in the day, she would be confronted with a mirror. She would stare at herself and say, "You look awful." She would then go back to bed if she could or continue on with the day feeling lower than before.

One of her assignments in therapy was to pay some attention to her appearance in the morning. She had to fix her hair, wear make-up, and put on clothing (other than pajamas or sweats). She quit experiencing the negative feelings when she looked in the mirror, thus reducing an element of her depression.

Our appearance can affect how we feel about ourselves. A helpful guideline is to think of how you would get ready in the morning if a friend or even the Lord were coming over to your house. Would you be comfortable or uncomfortable with your appearance?

Continue to put forth some effort where needed to make your appearance pleasing to your husband. In the process your husband will feel more loved and honored. You will make him feel special as you show him that he is worth dressing up for. He will be far less tempted to look elsewhere when he remembers who is waiting for him at home.

Notes

1. Dr. Arthur Szabo, quoted in *Bible Illustrator* on CD Rom (Hiawatha, IA: Parsons Technology, 1999).

If anyone does not provide for his relatives, and especially for his family, he has denied the faith and is worse than an unbeliever.

1 Timothy 5:8

5

A WIFE NEEDS HER HUSBAND'S
Protection and Provision

Attributes of Protection and Provision
- A husband should protect his wife against physical dangers
- A husband should protect his wife's time
- A husband should protect his wife from those who cause her emotional turmoil
- A husband should protect his wife and children from legal challenges
- A husband should provide the necessary finances or labor for the family's basic needs including housing, food, medical care, clothing, and transportation

*H*as your wife ever called you her knight in shining armor? Does she feel like a princess bride or a damsel in distress? Are you a chivalrous man or a cad? Webster describes chivalry as "the combination of qualities expected of a knight, including courage, generosity, and courtesy." Honorable men used to go to great lengths, perhaps to a fault, to protect the physical safety, honor, and dignity of women in general and their wives in particular.

Although you may no longer have the opportunity to wear armor and ride on horses, your wife needs the protection afforded by a chivalrous man as much now as any woman in history. She may not be in physical danger as often as a woman living on the frontier may have been, but there are other intrusions and dangers lurking in her life that need your assistance and protection.

Protecting Your Wife's Physical Safety

Relying on the Lord and praying for your family's protection is the ultimate safety barrier. But, it is presumptuous of us not to take the time and effort necessary to provide locks, safe vehicles, and big dogs (when appropriate) for our families as well. To maintain the safety of your family when they are at home and away from home, ask yourself three questions: *where*, *when*, and *who?*

1. Where?

Vickie is relatively unconcerned with her physical safety, and in the rural part of Virginia where we live her attitude is understandable. We do not take our safety for granted, however. Nowhere in America is one's physical safety guaranteed. Accordingly, we use the locks on our doors and have a 120-pound vigilant watchdog. When I travel, Vickie and the kids feel safe.

When Vickie ventures outside the safety of our home, I consider where she is going and caution her about possible concerns I may have. She often takes the kids into the Washington, D.C. area for field trips. By increasing her awareness of dangerous areas, she is better equipped to avoid places that might endanger her or the children.

2. When?

When I (Reed) get home from work, the last thing I want to do is leave my house and go to the grocery store. Yet Janine, who has been mothering and teaching all day at home, can't wait to get out of the house for a short time. I want to come home, relax, and leave the stress of the office outside my home. She wants to get out and away from home (her place of stress).

Sometimes she goes out on her own, and I stay home and watch the children. But increasingly we have found that even the neighborhood grocery store is not always safe at night. One evening, Janine walked out of the grocery store and some shady-looking characters followed her out of the store. She noticed they did not have any bags of groceries, and there were not any cars parked near ours in the parking lot. So she threw the groceries into the car, locked the doors, and zoomed off before she could find out what their intentions were. When Janine tells me of situations like this, I am reminded that I should leave the house with her at night. As her protector, it is my responsibility to make sure that she is safe at all times. Considering *when* my wife is going is just as important as considering *where* she is going.

3. Who?

When my counseling practice had a branch office in Peoria, Illinois, I would travel there one day a week for counseling sessions. One day I took Janine and my family with me to Peoria so we could do some shopping after I finished work. Janine took our children over to the mall to look around and kill time. After walking through the mall and stopping in a few stores, they came to the store that every parent dreads—the toy store. The kids were drawn into the store like matter sucked into a black hole (once you get within the pull of its gravity, it's almost impossible to get back out).

While in the toy store, she noticed a couple of suspicious characters hanging around outside the store. They seemed to be watching Janine and the children. Based on their dress and mannerisms, they did not appear to be truant officers. She began to keep an eye on them while she watched our children. When Janine and the kids left the toy store and continued walking through the mall, the men followed. The time for them to come and pick me up was approaching, but she was concerned that the two men might try to snatch one of our children in the parking lot. She waited until some other shoppers were leaving also and then left. It was after this incident that we decided that my duties as protector were not limited to *when* (such as nighttime) but needed to include *whom* she was with.

Protecting Your Wife's Time

Time is one of the most critical needs in the life of a home schooling wife and mother. She carries tremendous responsibilities and must make very careful use of this precious resource. Home schooling mothers lose time in so many ways.

The number one enemy of time is the telephone. A home schooling mom's daytime hours need to be primarily devoted to the instruction and training of her children. It is not her job to be the "Home School Answer-Woman" for every Thomasina, Dixie, and Harriet who calls. You know the routine:

Your wife answers the phone, "Hello."

"Hi, this is Harriet. I'm a friend of Suzy Smith, and she told me you are home schooling. I'm thinking of home schooling my children, and I'd like to ask you just a couple of questions."

Forty-five minutes later, Harriet's "couple" of questions finally wind to a close, and your wife has just shot a hole in her plans for the morning.

To escape lengthy telephone interruptions, answering machines are an absolute requirement for home schooling families to use during the school day. Scripture even backs up the use of answering machines: "Call if you will, but who will answer you?" (Job 5:1a) and, "Then they will call to Me but I will not answer; they will look for Me but will not find me" (Proverbs 1:28). I may have used these verses somewhat out of context, but you get the point.

Let your answering machine tell your callers, "I'm teaching and unable to come to the phone." You must also be considerate of others as well. Follow the Golden Rule and "Do unto others as you would have them do unto you" (Matthew 7:12). If you do not want people calling you during school time, do not call them either.

Some people think that home schooling homes are great places to drop their kids off in the middle of the day. They think, "After all, they're always home anyway." If your friends from church want to drop their kids off so they can go to Bible study, to the mall, or to the dentist, just say no.

If someone is sick in the hospital, we should be the first to help those who are truly in need. We need to differentiate between genuine crises (illnesses, accidents, hospitalizations, and deaths) and others minor crises of time or convenience. Our homes are primarily dedicated to the training of our children during daytime hours, and they shouldn't become the dumping grounds for those with more mobile lifestyles.

Men, if your wife has the gift of mercy and has a difficult time saying no to people who call or drop by, it is your job to protect her. Help her come up with some firm yet caring responses. For example, she could say, "I would be glad to watch your children as soon as my children have finished school for today." If necessary let her make you the bad guy. She could say, "I'm sorry but my husband doesn't like me to have other children over until our children have finished their school work." A home schooling husband needs to ensure that his wife's time is protected from "thieves" who would rob, steal, and destroy this precious resource.

Protecting Your Wife's Emotions

Home schooling families sometimes face a variety of "hassles." Relatives may not appreciate your home schooling and try to create difficulties. Neighbors can also cause a great deal of anxiety. Even people from your church can be a source of emotional turmoil if they do not approve of your home schooling. All of these particular hassles that confront some home schooling families exact a particular toll on the wife who feels her family is the target of the criticism.

When your wife faces one or more of these sources of emotional difficulty, it is your responsibility to intervene and provide the needed emotional protection. Become your wife's advocate. Find out who has been giving your wife the third degree about home schooling. See if you can answer some of the questions that person might have or share with him the latest research that shows the effectiveness of home schooling. Your goal is to satiate the person's curiosity, so he or she will leave your wife alone.

Your wife may face many other sources of turmoil that have nothing to do with home schooling. Regardless of the source of emotional stress, your responsibility is the same: protect your wife in a way that guards her emotions from "undue" stress.

No one can or should expect life to be absolutely free from stress. Simply being human requires a certain degree of give-and-take that creates some everyday emotional turmoil. A husband who tries to protect his wife from such normal turmoil will probably inappropriately offend others and arouse a negative response in his wife as well. For day-to-day trials, a husband's duty is simply to provide encouragement and comfort to his wife and to be a safe outlet for her to vent her feelings. Husbands need to exercise their listening skills at this point.

But when your wife faces turmoil and stress that crosses the line of normalcy, you should step in on her behalf. For example, if your wife's mother makes degrading comments about your family's choice of home schooling on a regular basis in a way that is clearly causing negative effects on either your wife or your children, then, men, it is your duty to intervene—even though she is *her* mother, not yours.

Your wife may strongly oppose the idea of you intervening with her relatives because she is afraid that you will not handle the confrontation appropriately. Many men know only one style of confrontation—all-out war. Rarely is this appropriate in any human interaction—but warfare is especially inappropriate when it comes to dealing with your relatives.

Gentle firmness is the style which a husband must master if he expects his wife to be willing to allow him to intervene on her behalf—especially with members of her own family. Meekness is the character trait he needs to exhibit.

When you think of *meekness,* what do you think of? Many people think of *weakness.* Actually, a meek person is a quiet, soft-spoken peacemaker. The Bible describes Moses as meek. It says, "Now the man Moses was very meek, above all the meekest which were upon the face of the earth" (Numbers 12:3 KJV).

Moses is not the first person who usually comes to mind when we think of a meek person because our understanding of the word *meek* is inaccurate. A better definition for *meekness* is *controlled strength*. Controlled strength is the ability to know you could have the last word in a discussion, but instead you realize that maintaining a relationship is more important than winning a discussion. Controlled strength is knowing that truth speaks loud enough on its own and does not need to be shouted or constantly repeated. Controlled strength is protecting your wife and family with firmness and gentleness.

My (Mike's) natural tendencies are to take out my "verbal" sword and lop off the head of anyone who "deserves" to be confronted. But I have slowly learned to consider my actions first. A few years ago, a stray dog in our yard was causing a series of problems. He got in our garage, knocked over the garbage can, and tore up the trash. More importantly, he was a real source of problems with our kids. He would steal the baby's bottle out of his hand and disappear with it. He would snatch hats off our boys' heads and run away. He even nipped at one of our girls. We were ready to call the humane society until we discovered he belonged to a new neighbor. Vickie wanted me to go talk to the neighbors about their dog, but she was initially worried that I might not handle the confrontation well. I comforted her fears by saying, "Don't worry, Vickie. I'll be nice. I want them to vote for me the next time I run for office."

That really satisfied her. If all men handled confrontations with the mindset of a politician who wants to win the hearts and minds of everyone, our wives would be much more comfortable with our commitment to gentle firmness. We shouldn't be unprincipled politicians who refuse to stand up for what is right by "wimping out" and declining to make necessary confrontations; however, when a confrontation is necessary we must try to accomplish our mission without rancor or anger.

If you develop the habit of gentle firmness, your wife will be thrilled for you to step in for her with any family, friend, neighbor, or church member who clearly crosses the line of civility and creates emotional turmoil in her life.

Protecting Your Wife from Legal Conflict

At Home School Legal Defense Association, we have handled dozens of legal situations for families where the wife has been in essence abandoned by her husband. We call a family in the late afternoon to follow-up on a situation, and the father answers the phone. Instead of talking with us himself, he says, "Just a minute, I'll get my wife. She's handling the legal situation."

Men, it's your responsibility to protect your wife and children. If there are legal confrontations related to your home schooling, your wife would greatly appreciate it if you were the one who conducted the bulk of the needed interaction with your lawyers and especially with any government officials.

Your responsibility to provide protection for your wife and children from legal conflicts requires, at a minimum, these steps:

- Review your state home schooling laws
- Take steps to comply with the laws consistent with your religious convictions
- Develop an adequate plan for the legal defense of your family

Home School Legal Defense Association is an excellent way for a husband to provide these needed attributes of legal protection for his family. But, the bottom line is not membership in HSLDA; it is taking any needed steps so that not only are you satisfied with your situation, but you have also satisfied your wife's need for confidence and security.

For more information on the home schooling laws in your state, and a membership application for the Home School Legal Defense Association write to Home School Legal Defense Association, P.O. Box 3000, Purcellville, Virginia 20132 or call (540) 338-5600 or www.hslda.org.

Abram's Negative Example of Protection

In Genesis 12, we read the sad story of Abram's (whom God would later call Abraham) selfish refusal to protect his wife Sarai (Sarah). As they were entering Egypt, Abram told Sarai,

I know what a beautiful woman you are. When the Egyptians see you, they will say, "This is his wife." Then they will kill me but will let you live. Say you are my sister, so that I will be treated well for your sake and my life will be spared because of you. (Genesis 12:11-13)

Abram's lack of protection showed great selfishness. Not only was he willing to allow Sarai to be sexually ravished by the Egyptians, but he was willing to leave her in Egypt as the wife or concubine of an Egyptian.

His attitude was the same as the hiker in an old joke. Two hikers confronted a grizzly bear on a trail. The first hiker immediately sat down on the trail and started pulling off his hiking boots and putting on his tennis shoes. The second hiker said, "You know you can't outrun a grizzly bear. They're faster than a horse." The first hiker replied, "I don't have to outrun the bear, I just have to outrun you."

Abram thought if he could just "outwit" the Egyptians, he would spare his life, even if it meant losing Sarai. His selfishness had long-range consequences. The sins of Abram were passed down to the third and fourth generation (Exodus 34:7). His son, Isaac, imitated the same scenario when he and his wife, Rebecca, went to live among the Philistines during a famine (Genesis 26). The family trait of lying for convenience sake was also passed down to Jacob. Jacob's name literally means *deceiver*. It is likely that Lot, Abram's nephew who grew up in Abram's household, knew about this incident as well. Where did Lot come up with the idea to give up his daughters to the mob of perverts in Sodom? We have already seen the long-range consequences of Lot's actions.

Moreover, Abram not only had a callous attitude toward his wife, but he showed utter disdain for the covenant of God. God had promised to bless Abram with a family that would grow into a mighty nation. This would presumptively occur through a faithful relationship with his wife. Giving his wife up to the Egyptians demonstrated that Abram felt preserving his life was more important than protecting his wife and obeying God.

The main reason men fail to protect their wives is usually a result of selfishness. Our duty to protect our wives' time, emotions, physical safety, and legal needs should not be neglected by our selfishness or indifference. Ultimately, failing to protect our wives shows disdain for the God who has given them to us as a precious gift.

Providing for Your Family's Needs

Most men recognize their need to be the one who supplies the financial income for the family. Some exceptions to this rule involve the physical incapacity of the husband. But unless you are disabled, laid up in a full body cast, or some equivalent circumstance, it is your responsibility to meet the financial needs of your family.

We live in an age where there is an assumption that both husband and wife will work—at least after the point in life when all the children of the family have become school age. Obviously, Christian home schooling families have decided to arrange their lives in a way that directly challenges this assumption. Moms are committed to staying home with their children to raise them and teach them. There is an underlying assumption that goes with the decision to become a home schooling father: such a man has committed himself to becoming the sole means of support for his family. One excuse I hear often from husbands is, "I can't afford for my wife to stay home with the kids." What they are really saying is, "I can't afford our lifestyle if my wife stays home with the kids."

Home schooling fathers who have made the choice to be the only source of income for the family usually do not question their need to provide for their families in the areas of housing, food, clothing, or transportation. But one area that many let slide is medical care. Medical coverage has become a necessity in today's world. It is not an option if you want to protect your family from a potential financial crisis.

One family without healthcare found themselves with a million dollar debt after their son was hit by a car and received a series of brain operations. The son died ten days later, despite all of the doctors' heroic efforts. His parents were left with a bill they would never be able to repay. The hospital eventually reduced their debt to $60,000, but even then the parents were unable to pay it. They were forced into bankruptcy as a result of their choice to forgo medical coverage. Not only were they devastated by the loss of their youngest child, but also they were left with financial repercussions that would haunt them for many years to come.

If you do not have a medical plan in place that protects your family, get one. One solution is to get a better job that provides such benefits. Another option is to join a program like the Christian Brotherhood Newsletter or

Samaritan Ministries Christian Health Care Newsletter. These organizations are made up of Christians who have mutually pledged to share the burden in paying one another's medical bills. The plans are similar to the way insurance works, but there are also some distinct differences. Nonetheless, they provide an organized plan for paying your medical bills in a responsible way. We are members of one of the plans mentioned, and we have found that the program works. We are simply "bearing one another's burden" (Galatians 6:2).

When I (Mike) was in private legal practice, I was in a partnership with two other Christian attorneys. We had a number of clients who professed to be born-again Christians who came to us because they wanted a "Christian lawyer." It did not take long to discover that what they really wanted was a free lawyer. As a young lawyer I was making around $12,000 a year—we were barely making it. But I had $40,000 in unpaid fees, largely from Christian clients. They had faith that God would supply their needs, but their financial priorities rarely included paying me. When I had a new client, I felt that if the person made no profession of faith I was more likely to be paid.

A Christian should not walk into a doctor's office uninsured and say, "I will pay you at some future date when God supplies my financial needs." He forces the doctor to make a loan without his consent. A Christian does not honor our Lord when he owes money that he is unable to promptly pay to a doctor or hospital upon terms that are agreeable to them. Christians who fail or refuse to pay their bills defame the name of our Lord Jesus Christ. This is true of all bills, including our medical expenses.

The government is not responsible for the medical needs of your family either. Nor are doctors and hospitals responsible for providing your family's medical needs. Provision for medical care is your responsibility. Get yourself insured, save up enough money to cover medical emergencies, or become a member of a mutual payment plan.

Hindrances to the Duty to Provide

Every husband initially desires to provide well for his family. But sometimes along the way, his good intentions get muddled. Let's look at eight hindrances that often keep a man from providing the best for his family:

1. Pride

If a man is laid off from a good job for which he has training and experience, it is very appropriate for him to spend some time trying to find a new job that is similar or perhaps even a little better. But after a while, if he is unable to find work "in his field," then he simply needs to find work in another field, even if it means taking a lower position or salary. He can always continue to look for work after he has accepted a job that does not quite meet his career desires.

His financial circumstances will determine how long he can remain unemployed. But at some point in time, he needs to find employment even if he still has money in the bank. Within three or four months, perhaps six months at the most, a man normally should be able to find a job that is somewhat related to his previous job. If he cannot find a job that meets his criteria within that period, then he should take a job wherever he can find one. Flipping burgers at McDonald's is not out of the question. He may even have to work two jobs until he can find the job that meets his financial needs. Whatever he can find to bridge the financial gap is more appropriate than sitting at home waiting for the phone to ring from that mystery employer who is going to offer him the perfect job. The longer he sits at home, the more "undue" stress he heaps on his wife. If this describes you, swallow your pride and get to work.

2. Laziness

Some men simply do not like to work. Self-employment is a great concept if someone is actually making some money at it. But, if after a reasonable period a person is still not making an adequate living, self-employment is probably just a scheme of creative laziness. There is nothing wrong with a man who wants to succeed through his own business, but if his motivation is "I don't like other people telling me what to do," he is not very likely to succeed and may be masking his own rebelliousness.

3. Big talk, little action

Some men do not provide adequately for their families; but when they talk about their dreams and schemes, one would suppose they were Wall Street tycoons. Talk is cheap, but action requires sacrifice and commitment. A man who talks of dreams and schemes but goes to work at a minimum wage job is all talk and no action. If your talk and your dreams are so unrealistic that they cannot produce any improved financial reality for your family, get yourself a new set of dreams.

One man who struggled financially came with his wife to see me (Reed) for marriage counseling. His wife was bright and beautiful, and they had great children. "Andy" talked a great talk. But after I asked him just a few questions, it was evident that his family problems were largely bound up in his financial woes. He simply had unrealistic dreams and would not make realistic plans. His wife later divorced him. Consequently, she had to go to work and give up home schooling. Her husband's inability to provide for his family caused the breakup of their marriage.

I have known other men who have perfectly good ideas and realistic notions, but they simply refuse to act on their dreams. The security of a minimal job has served as an anchor when they needed to fly. Security is fine. But when security becomes a harbor for fear, it has served to keep many a good idea tied at the dock of insufficiency. Set realistic goals and pursue them.

4. No dreams, little action

Some men languish on the border of poverty with no real hope of ever changing their life circumstances. America is still the land of opportunity for those willing to work hard. It takes surprisingly little to rise above the average these days. In many cases you are stuck because your vision is stuck. Dream a little. Pray a lot. And set your sights higher.

If you are stuck in an insufficient job, use creativity, hard work, and prayer to come up with a life plan that has more opportunity. Find a man in your church or home school support group who has achieved a degree of business success and ask him to talk with you about how you could improve your ability to earn a livelihood for your family. Make sure he understands that you are coming to him for counsel only and not for a loan or a job. Working sixteen hours a day is not a good solution, but some additional work may well be warranted. But don't forget, you cannot begin to meet the needs of your wife and children if you are never around.

This advice to work harder and devote more time to providing for your family is only intended for those who are struggling financially because of very low incomes. If you are struggling financially because of debt, wild spending, or other forms of irresponsibility, the main cure is not "work harder" but spend less money. The vast number of men make adequate salaries. Their family's greatest need is more time with dad. But, if you are one of those who are simply living on the margins of life, set your sights a little higher, get some advice, and get to work.

5. Failing to manage resources

Most of us make enough money to cover the basics, but we still struggle with certain aspects of our finances.

These struggles can produce uncertainty and tension between a husband and wife.

My basic struggle is time. I (Mike) have so many things to do in life, that I feel like I just don't have adequate time to change the filters on the heat pumps every six months, keep the interior of my house painted regularly (and with ten kids you can just imagine that painting is necessary from time to time), and balance the checkbook promptly. My secondary struggle is lack of interest. I really have no talent whatsoever for home maintenance projects and only slightly more interest than talent. My failure to take care of a ten-dollar, three-hour maintenance project can end up costing me hundreds of dollars in major repairs later on.

If you have adequate resources, there is nothing inherently wrong with hiring help to do certain aspects of routine maintenance. But unless you are a multi-millionaire with a live-in maintenance man, every one of us is going to have to engage in a certain amount of maintenance. If you can't afford to hire someone and you do not know how, go to the library. The library has "how to" videos and step-by-step books for any kind of maintenance work. Ask an expert. Find someone in your church or home school community who can talk you through a project if you get stuck.

Some men let money slip through their fingers. Bills that are paid on time do not incur late fees. Health insurance claims, which are submitted for reimbursement, get reimbursed—those that sit in your drawer are never reimbursed.

Many years ago, Fram Filters had a TV commercial that showed an auto mechanic handing someone a several hundred dollar estimate for a blown engine which was caused by failing to install a new, preferably Fram, oil filter. His pitch was, "You can pay me now or pay me later." Maintenance is unavoidable. You can either take care of small problems or pay for large problems later. Procrastination has its price.

Your wife's opinion of your willingness to meet her needs will dramatically improve if you take care of home maintenance and financial management in a timely manner.

6. Robbing God

Once sure way to guarantee that you will have financial difficulties is to rob God. What does it mean to rob God? The Lord tells us clearly,

> "Will a man rob God? Yet you rob Me.
> "But you ask, 'How do we rob You?'
> "In tithes and offerings. You are under a curse—the whole nation of you—because you are robbing Me. Bring the whole tithe into the storehouse, that there may be food in My house. Test Me in this," says the Lord Almighty, "and see if I will not throw open the floodgates of heaven and pour out so much blessing that you will not have enough room for it." (Malachi 3:8-10)

The Old Testament tithe is not a legalistic mandate to us in the New Testament age, but it is an example of what God expects. We gravely misunderstand the nature of the example if the "law of love" does not compel us to set our goal to match the tithe or perhaps even do better. Regardless of one's exact doctrinal views on giving, which vary to some degree among solid believers, there is no variance on the consequences of robbing God. If we do not follow through with the giving that we have "purposed in our hearts" (Daniel 1:8) to give to the Lord, we are going to see serious financial consequences as a result.

It may seem strange to the outside world, but the reality is this: your wife will be blessed and feel more satisfied with you as a husband and leader if you faithfully devote an appropriate portion of your income to go back to the Lord. As with any major decision in life, I would strongly recommend that you consult with your wife in setting your family's goal in giving. But ultimately, the responsibility and decision resides with you.

7. "Get-rich-quick" schemes

The summer before Vickie and I got married, I was invited to a "money-making opportunity" meeting. A very large crowd gathered in the hotel ballroom. The room was buzzing with talk and enthusiasm. But the crowd became absolutely electrified when a man in a fiery orange polyester jumpsuit with gold chains (it *was* 1971) ran down the center aisle as the insiders in the crowd yelled, "Monnneeeey!"

I soon discovered that I could become rich beyond my wildest dreams if I paid them $10,000 to join their scheme. All I had to do to be a "salesman" was pay them $10,000 and then ask all my friends to give me $10,000 so they too could become "salesmen." The guy in the orange suit would get an appropriate percentage, of course. The only thing you sold was the right to become salesmen—no products were involved. This was a classic (and quite illegal) pyramid scheme. Since I was only nineteen, they suggested I borrow the money from my parents "to not miss this grand opportunity to make triple that amount in a week or two."

I declined. But, that night I watched a lot of "mature" adults sign mortgages on their homes to get their $10,000 on the line before it was too late. "Get-rich" schemes sometimes work for the person who thinks them up, like the man in the orange suit. But normally, he ends up in jail. If you conceive a legal "get-rich-quick" scheme of your own, it probably will not result in your getting rich.

Some Christians believe all Christians are supposed to be rich to show that they are blessed. Some Christians say all Christians are supposed to be poor to show that they are virtuous. None of these extremes makes you a better Christian necessarily, but the Bible does say that Christian dads are to meet the basic needs of their families (1 Timothy 5:8).

There is nothing wrong with getting rich slowly— especially if it is the result of hard work or innovative ideas. One may have a single good idea that propels him ahead in a very rapid manner. This occurrence is rare, but it does happen. Normally, it is the result of years of work or training that suddenly results in a flash of insight that proves to be very profitable. The key to getting rich in such cases was not merely the flash of insight, but the years of hard work that preceded it.

For most of us, we will have happier wives and stabler lives if our financial goals are organized around a time schedule that produces steady but sure financial growth.

8. Premature marriage

Proverbs 24:27 says, "Finish your outdoor work early and get your fields ready; after that, build your house." This verse teaches one of the most important principles concerning courtship: A man should get his livelihood in order and after that he should get married and start his family. A young man is not ready to *begin* the process of courtship until he is financially ready to support his family.

Vickie and I violated this principle. We got married between our sophomore and junior year in college. I had already decided to become a lawyer, so we entered the marriage with the plan that I would go to school for five more years before I would begin to work full-time to support my family. Vickie's parents had enough money set aside to finish paying her way through the last two years of college. Between scholarships, student loans, and part-time jobs, I was able to support my own education and our minimal living expenses.

After we graduated from college, we had planned on Vickie getting a full-time teaching job to support our family as I went to law school. The sovereignty of God intervened in a number of ways to frustrate our plans. He guided us toward a biblical family design.

First of all, Vickie couldn't find a teaching job. It seemed that among other problems, there was a glut of law wives wanting to teach school. Second, Vickie got pregnant during my second year in law school and so even her "make do" job in a photo store came to an end. My plan to attend a "prestige" law school as a full-time day student was also deterred. I was on the waiting list for a couple of such schools, but I also applied to Gonzaga Law School as an optional school I could attend if the others did not work out in time.

Applying to Gonzaga turned out to be a great blessing in disguise. I had applied to Gonzaga so late in the process that I was admitted to their evening program rather than the day course. Because I attended school in the evening, I was able to work during the day to support my family. My second and third years of law school were spent working thirty hours a week in a law firm. I was able to try a number of cases before I ever graduated.

The day after I passed the bar and was sworn in as a lawyer, I began a weeklong real estate fraud jury trial and won. My firm never would have let me take the case if I had graduated from a prestige school and had no practical trial experience in the prior two years. Working in the firm allowed me to begin the process of supporting my family a lot sooner than I had intended. I did not make enough to pay for school entirely, so I

continued to borrow heavily for student loans (a decision I also regret). But I am very grateful that God
directed our paths toward a godly family pattern early
in our marriage.

God was gracious and merciful to Vickie and me. In
our ignorance He blessed us and yet He also allowed us
to face the consequences of some of our poor decisions.
I did not understand the Biblical concept of courtship. I
did not know that a man and woman should avoid
romantic relationships until the season of life when they
are prepared to be married and support a family.

Vickie's parents wanted us to wait a while to get married. They were concerned about how we would support
ourselves through college and law school. Being young
and in love, I tended to dismiss her dad's arguments
because I thought her dad's biblical knowledge (which
dramatically increased in later years) was minimal at the
time. Now I know that his common sense was not only
good common sense, but also in full harmony with the
Word of God. (I also know the danger of ignoring the
counsel of your wife's father, regardless of his spiritual
perspective). My relationship with my in-laws was difficult for a good while because I did not pay attention to
their advice. My relationship with Vickie was also
strained at times because I violated God's design for
marriage by getting married before I was able to support
my family.

Time, gracious in-laws, and a repentant heart heal
many wounds. My later "success" does not justify my
early errors lest someone feel tempted to repeat them. If

I had been told that I couldn't begin courtship until I passed the bar exam, I would have hustled through college and law school a year or two sooner if I had known that Vickie was the prize at the end of the trail.

Since the audience of this book is couples who are already married, our point is not to help you decide whether you are prepared for marriage. Our present goal should be to chart a plan for the future.

What do you do now if you are suffering financial consequences from a premature marriage?

First, go before God and confess the *timing* of your marriage as sin. It is God's will that you be married to your wife. Do not use this issue as an excuse to engage in mind games: "I wonder whom I would have married if I had waited until I was ready to be married?" That thought pattern is nothing more than sophisticated mental adultery.

Next, ask your wife to forgive you for violating God's standards and for not being properly prepared to support her when you married her. She didn't sin—you did.

Then decide to take steps of resolution, which do not involve sending your wife to work. The consequences you face as a result of a premature marriage are your problem and your responsibility.

It took me about fifteen years to fully pull out of the financial consequences caused by my premature marriage. It was a long haul, but a life lesson that has made us wiser. You can be guaranteed that my sons and daughters are being instructed toward scrupulously avoiding premature marriage.

God judges our hearts first. If we get our hearts right before Him, He will be gracious and begin to bless us with solutions to our problems.

Following God's Leading

In 1982, I had to make a decision about whether or not to move from Washington State to the Washington, D.C. area. Naturally, I wanted to determine what God's will was for my life. During this period of time, someone told me the following joke:

> A man was caught in his home during a flood. As the waters rose to a knee-high level, a man in a canoe paddled by. The man in the canoe, stopped and yelled, "Come on, buddy. Get in. This flood is going to get bad."
>
> The man declined saying, "No thanks. God is going to save me."
>
> The flood continued to rise and covered the entire first floor of his home. The man was leaning out his second-floor window when a power-boat came by. Again the offer was made, "Come on, friend. Get in!"
>
> Again the man declined saying, "No thanks. God is going to save me."
>
> Finally, he was perched on his roof when a helicopter crew spotted him. Over the loud-speaker came the inevitable words, "Grab the robe, and we'll pull you in!"
>
> "No thanks," he shouted back. "God is going to save me!"

Waiting for God to save him, the man drowned. In heaven, he shortly met God. "God," he said, "I relied on you to save me and I drowned. What happened?"

God replied, "It's your own fault. After all, I sent you a canoe, a power boat, and a helicopter."

Although I primarily relied on more traditional sources, that joke helped me make the decision about whether or not to move. In Washington State, I was the head of a non-profit legal foundation that was simply unable to pay my salary. In Washington, D.C. I had a job offer to run the Washington office of Concerned Women for America, and I would receive a steady paycheck. God's will for me was clear: I was to go where I could support my family.

If you are struggling to earn a living in the community you are in— go where the jobs are. I place a high premium on relationships with extended family. But if you are living near extended family, but cannot support your immediate family, you have to take care of your first priority.

Misunderstanding God's Will in Ministry

As Hudson Taylor lived by faith as a missionary in China, God abundantly provided for him again and again. George Mueller lived by faith as he ran an orphanage, and God faithfully provided for his needs time and again. I know other people who have placed themselves in ministry positions and have proceeded to live by faith, but in their situations, God's supernatural provision has not been evident. What's going on? Why does God provide for some ministries or missionaries and not for others?

The simple explanation is where God guides, He provides. What God truly orders, He pays for. One of the best indicators of whether or not God wants a particular person to pursue a certain ministry is whether or not the funds are there to pay for it.

If you are pastoring a church, and it requires your full-time efforts, you should be receiving a full-time wage from your church. If you are unable to meet the needs of your family, and this situation has persisted for six months or more, you should begin to seriously question if God wants you in this ministry. Every difficult situation in the ministry is not an attack from the enemy. Sometimes God is trying to get our attention. If this situation has persisted for a couple of years or more, you can be virtually guaranteed that God does *not* want you in that ministry. If, as a pastor, you have floated from church to church and the situation of unmet needs follows you year after year wherever you go, you need to face the fact that God probably does not want you in the pastorate at all.

In home schooling circles, a lot of men desire to go into full-time service running some form of home education ministry. If this is God's will for you, you will get paid a decent living. Short tests of faith are often appropriate. Prolonged, failing experiments are not based on faith but are simply a refusal to recognize the will of God in your life.

You're Not Alone

To provide for your family and protect them from harm is your responsibility as a husband. But God does not leave you alone to wander aimlessly in the dark as you undertake this task. He is Jehovah-Jireh, the ultimate provider of your needs. He is there waiting for you to ask Him, "Lord, what would You have me do?" Practice your listening skills.

It is not good for man to be alone.

Genesis 2:18

6

A HUSBAND NEEDS HIS WIFE'S

Companionship
and Mature Love

Attributes of companionship:
- A wife should be her husband's friend
- A wife should play with her husband

Attributes of mature love:
- Mature love builds self-discipline on top of emotional love

*T*he Lord God said, "It is not good for man to be alone. I will make a helper suitable for him" (Genesis 2:18). God created woman to be man's companion, a helpmate.

Jewish tradition interprets the creation of Adam and Eve like this: When God made Adam, He made him in

His image, complete, lacking nothing. When God put Adam to sleep and took out the rib to make Eve, He also removed part of His characteristics. Adam was no longer complete as an individual. Eve possessed part of God's characteristics. Adam needed her to feel complete.

While this tradition may not be explicitly found in Scripture (and God noted that even as initially created it was not good for man to be alone), there is little doubt about the basic point of this story: men need the companionship of women.

Just as Eve made Adam complete, a man and woman united in marriage also complete each other. Together they become stronger than they were alone. Often a man and woman are attracted to each other's differences. These differences make them stronger together than if they were apart. A husband's strengths may be his wife's weaknesses, and a wife's strengths may be her husband's weaknesses. When the couple learns how to combine their strengths to overcome their weaknesses, they will have a powerful union as they seek to be helpmates to each other.

Choices

How do a husband and wife develop a powerful union? By making choices that are other-centered rather than self-centered. Women are bombarded every day with opportunities to make the wrong choice. Today we are led to believe a woman has many options if she is unhappy in her marriage. Here are some ideas that the world recommends:

1. Get a job

The world says: "Work outside the home and put your children in daycare or school. This way someone else can raise them while you surround yourself by people who will tell you how great you are and what a good job you do. Don't worry about your family's needs; they can take care of themselves."

2. Get a divorce

The world says: "You only live life once so you might as well make yourself as happy as you can. You are doing all the work anyway since your husband isn't supportive, so life would be easier without the bum. Forget that divorce usually means a reduction in income and lifestyle for the family. Forget that about one-third of fathers are involved in their children's lives for the first year, and less as the years go on."

3. Have an affair

The world says: "There are plenty of men out there that will tell you that you are beautiful, incredible, or talented. If you want romance, you won't find it staying married. Maybe there is someone better out there for you. Don't worry about all the pain this will bring your family."

4. Go back to school

The world says: "If you are unsatisfied as a mother, go back to school and get a degree. Then you will be able to start a career and make a lot of money. Never mind the fact that two-thirds of women with master's degrees are leaving the work force to stay home with their families."

5. Wait until the kids leave the nest

The world says: "If you don't want to harm your children's future, then just stick around until all the children are raised and then leave your husband. You can make a fresh start on your own."

6. Become a nag

The world says: "Complain to your husband everyday in hopes that eventually he will hear you and shape up. Never mind the tension and hostility your words will breed."

The world's choices promise fulfillment but deliver emptiness. Finding a new husband, a new job, a new future will not make you happier if you disobey God's principles. The world's methods always seek to fulfill self. The problem with the flesh is that it is never satisfied. No matter how hard you try, without the Spirit of Christ filling you up each day, you will remain empty.

The messages I (Reed) hear and see in my counseling office come in many different disguises, but persistently they are focused on self. The excuses sound like this: "I can't stand it anymore. It's not fair." Or, "No one else has to put up with what I am going through. And besides, I don't love him anymore." All these are variants of "me-isms."

When you hear "me-isms" creeping into your thought-life, kick them out. These thoughts need to be put out of your mind. In 1 Corinthians 2:16b we are told to "have the mind of Christ." Ask the Lord to show you how He sees your husband. Ask Him to give you compassion for your husband in place of judgment.

Remember those vows you took on your wedding day? For better or worse, for richer or poorer, in sickness and in health—the vows you said yes to were not multiple choice. You said yes to all of them. You may be thinking now, "But I didn't know he really would become worse, poor, and sick!"

Hang on to the Lord and hang in there with your husband until you have the marriage God promised you. A pastor once made the point that God does not answer prayer like *The Little Engine That Could* saying, "I think I can. I think I can. I think I can." God says, "Yes, Yes, and Amen!" to our prayers. We have to exercise a little patience sometimes because His answer is not always how we think it should be done or on our time schedule.

God desires for you and your husband to have a great marriage. He desires for you to be a unified, winning team. The success of your team depends on the choices you make each day. As you make choices, remember that self-fulfillment is not the goal; self-sacrifice is. The world will always tell you, "Do whatever makes you happy." But God will say, "Do what makes Me happy, and I will give you the desires of your heart" (Matthew 6:33).

The world competes for your attention. The feminists' movement always desires one more convert. The feminists' agenda has even crept into the church. (Read Mary Pride's, *The Way Home.*) Only God can really tell you what is best for you. He will not compete with the clamor of other voices. He still speaks in a still small voice (1 Kings 19:12-13) and through His Word (2 Timothy 3:16, Romans 10:17).

Play with Your Husband

When you were a kid, what did you do with your best friend? More than likely you played together. In high school you probably played together in a different way than when you were kids, but you still knew how to have fun. As married couples, we can't forget to make playtime a priority. Adults need to play just as much as kids do.

During a marriage counseling session, one wife began telling me (Reed) how she dreaded hunting season. She explained, "I always feel abandoned during the fall because my husband is always out hunting. Shooting a silly deer is more important to him than I am."

"When you were dating, what did you do together?" I asked.

"Oh," she smiled, "we did everything together."

"What were your husband's interests then?"

"Well, we went fishing and hiking, bowling, to car shows, and he even taught me how to shoot a bow and arrow."

"How much of that do you do together now?"

"None" she replied.

As we continued to talk, she realized he had given up several of his past interests as their family had grown so he could be home with the family. He did not fish unless it was with their children. He did not go on weeklong trips to Montana to hunt for elk or other big game. He even quit playing in softball leagues. Hunting deer near his home was about the only thing left that he was still actively involved in. As we talked further, she admitted that hunting seasons were usually short, a couple of weeks at a time throughout the year.

We came up with a plan that would make both partners happy. She arranged for the children to stay with the relatives, and the following weekend when her husband went out to scout for a place to put up his tree stand, she went with him.

When I saw them the next week, they were both beaming. Her husband said it felt like old times when they used to go hiking together. She had made a picnic lunch that they had thrown in a backpack and taken with them. They had a wonderful day together away from phones, children, home schooling, the office, and the housework. They had time to talk and listen to each other. He had even agreed to go to a craft show with her on a Saturday after hunting season was over. Their love for each other was rekindled as she entered her husband's world and became his companion again.

Perhaps I knew that my suggestion would work because Janine has regularly shown me her love by going camping with me. When I was growing up, my family used to go camping together. I was active in Boy Scouts, so I also did quite a bit of hiking and camping with my troop. My wife was active in Girl Scouts, but her hiking and camping experiences were far different from mine.

I had grown up on the East Coast and spent outings camping and hiking in the Appalachian Mountains for days or weeks at a time. My wife had grown up in California in the Los Angeles area. One of her camping experiences had been at a campground that overlooked Hollywood. While the girls roasted marshmallows and sang around the fire, Patty Hearst was being held hostage by kidnappers in an abandoned bomb shelter nearby. (Of course, they did not find this out until after they got home.) Another Girl Scout camping trip was at a Union Carbide plant located in the city. There was a beautiful park area where they camped, but a high chain-link fence topped with barbed wire to "keep the crazies out" surrounded the plant.

Even though my wife enjoyed camping, she had certain fears to overcome. Early in our marriage when we lived in Missouri, we decided to go camping. Our campsite was near the road, which I later discovered was not the best of places. During the night cars drove by and lit up our tent with their headlights. As each car passed, Janine feared someone would take random shots at our tent. Needless to say, she was not a happy camper by the time morning finally came around.

It took some time for Janine to feel safe while camping and to learn how to get a good night's sleep in a tent. Her motivation to be with me and to be my companion compelled her to go with me on many more camping trips over the years. Is she as enthused about camping as I am? No, but her willingness to be by my side (even sleeping in a tent) has strengthened our friendship. After sixteen years of camping we are happy to report that we have never been shot at yet.

Treat your husband like you would treat a best friend, and you will see a change in your relationship. What do best friends do? They listen and talk to each other about anything and everything. They don't make judgments about the other's opinions, feelings, and tastes. They do things together and go places together that may or may not be of mutual interest.

Often I see a difference between how we treat our spouses and how we treat our friends. Spouses usually are on the short end of the stick. Don't let familiarity breed contempt in your marriage. Find ways to keep your marriage fresh. Nurture your friendship. Do fun things together like you did when you were dating. Depending on how many children you have and how accessible babysitters are will determine how and where you play. But by all means, don't let kids stop you from having fun. You just have to be more creative.

Ladies, your husband wants a companion. He can fill the gap with his buddies or a dog, but they are just substitutes for you. God made him with a need for a companion that only you can fill.

Choose God's Way

Even though the culture has tried to rewrite the role of women in the home, we don't have to accept their new version. Titus 2:3-5 clearly describes a wife's role:

> Likewise, teach the older women to be reverent in the way they live, not to be slanderers or addicted to much wine, but to teach what is

good. Then they can train the younger women to love their husbands and children, to be self-controlled and pure, to be busy at home, to be kind, and to be subject to their husbands, so that no one will malign the word of God.

When Titus read Paul's letter to the women of Crete, how do you think they reacted? Did they like the idea of being subject to their husbands? What inspired Paul to say what he did? Were the women out of control and addicted to wine when he last met with them? Since we were not there, we can only guess what the Cretans' reactions were to his message. If the pagan culture that surrounded the Cretans was anything like the secular culture that surrounds us today, Paul's advice may have been antithetical to their culture's values as well.

The opposition to biblical values will always be present no matter what culture we live in, so we must rise above the values of our age and accept God's values.

Older Women and Younger Women

As Paul addressed the older women, he reinforced the concept that the older should teach the younger not only by their words but also by their actions. In this way godly values would be handed down from one generation to the next.

During one couple's fiftieth wedding anniversary celebration, some of the younger women at the party surrounded the honored wife in the kitchen and asked her this question:

"What is your secret? How have you stayed married for fifty years?"

The woman paused as she thought about the secret of their success. Then she said to the younger women, "On my wedding day I made a list of ten things that my husband-to-be did that bothered me. I vowed to myself that anytime he did something on the list, I would ignore it or forgive him and go on."

The younger women marveled at the simple cleverness of her secret. The older woman broke into a sly grin and confessed, "I really never did make a list of ten things, but anytime he did anything that annoyed me I told myself, 'Good thing that's on the list!' and went on."

The wife's choice to look past his annoyances and forgive as necessary was a major contributor to the longevity of her marriage. She chose to love the way God loves us. She chose to love her husband unconditionally, in spite of his faults. She followed the biblical standard of love. Romans 5:8 says, "While we were still sinners, Christ died for us." God did not wait until we were good enough to send Christ. He sent Christ because we were so bad. He loved us in spite of our weaknesses. Unconditional love sees past what we are today and looks forward to what we will become. A wife who loves her husband unconditionally will inspire him to become a man of character.

Young wives, find an older woman who has a "Ph.D." in Titus 2:3-5, a woman whose life will give you an example to follow. Find a woman who has wisdom and credibility to give you godly counsel and train you to do the following:

1. Love your husband as a committed friend

When you were first married, you may have at some point realized the honeymoon was over. You questioned yourself, "What have I done? Who is this man I married? How will I love him for the rest of my life?" Developing a love for a lifetime does not happen overnight. It is a process of learning how to forgive and forget over and over again. It means learning how to be a true friend. According to Titus 2:4, younger women should love (*philandros*) their husbands. The Greek word *philandros* means "to be a friend."

We have a small plaque that I gave to Janine when we were first married. We have hung the plaque above the kitchen sink in every home we have lived in so we would see it often. The plaque has a hand-painted picture of a bride and groom all dressed up for their wedding day on it and the saying, "Happiness is being married to your best friend." The plaque reminds us daily that marriage is a friendship. We try to become better friends every day.

In Bible days couples did not marry because they were "in love." Most marriages were arranged by their parents. Over time, emotional attachments naturally developed between a husband and wife. Commitment came first and emotion followed.

Our society has it backward. We emotionally attach ourselves to our marriage partners and then hope commitment will follow. The problem with basing our commitments solely on our emotions is that emotions are fickle. When people treat us right, we are happy. When people treat us wrong, we want to get even. A marriage based on emotion alone will not last for long.

When your alarm clock goes off in the morning your emotions may say, "Hit the snooze button." You may do that several times until your mind says, "You must get up! You have responsibilities and commitments to attend to today." Your actions kick in, and you get up and go about your day. If you had listened only to your emotions, you would have slept until you could sleep no more. You would have felt refreshed when you finally woke up, but a feeling of guilt about the work you had neglected would soon replace your pleasant mood, especially if you were penalized at work because of your laziness.

Your feelings give you pleasure for a time, but when they are given free reign, they can lead to trouble. Controlling your emotions takes practice. Just like the tongue is compared to a fire that can rapidly spread destruction (James 3:6), your emotions can also wreak havoc in your life if they are not controlled.

Scripture tells us to control our emotions by practicing a pure thought life:

Finally, brothers, whatever is true, whatever is noble, whatever is right, whatever is pure, whatever is lovely, whatever is admirable—if anything is excellent or praiseworthy—think about those things. (Philippians 4:8)

If I tell someone to feel happy when he leaves my office, he may try to follow my advice, but it may be difficult for him to conjure up that emotion. If I tell him as he leaves to think about a happy occasion, such as a holiday gathering or birthday party, he will eventually crack a smile and notice some happy or joyful feelings.

What does all of this have to do with loving your husband? Focus on loving thoughts and actions toward your husband, and loving feelings will follow. If you think about your husband's strengths throughout the day, you will have positive feelings toward him when he gets home from work. If you dwell on his negative traits throughout the day, you will be ready to pounce on him with criticism when he walks in the door.

Practicing loving thoughts and actions toward your husband is a win-win situation. You will gain loving feelings toward him, and even if you don't feel better you still win. How do you win? You win because you have nothing to feel guilty or ashamed of when you stand before God. Your thoughts and actions are obedient to His ways. The feelings you would be judged by (bitterness, envy, and unforgiveness) are not present. It may sound silly, but try this method: act until it is a fact. Loving feelings do follow loving thoughts and actions. Love is a decision.

2. Love your husband as a kind friend

Have a cheerful spirit. Remember Ephesians 4:32, "Be kind and compassionate to one another, forgiving each other, just as in Christ God forgave you." At times being a home schooling mom is a thankless job. You may get frustrated and discouraged with how your school day, school year, or even how your life is going. Try to focus on what you are doing well instead. When you are smiling on the inside, it is easier to smile on the outside.

When you are not smiling on the inside it may be because your challenges seem bigger than your ability to conquer them. This is when you need to go to the well (Jesus) and get refreshed by His living water. Take some time for yourself. Find a place of solitude to get away from the challenges you face. Ask your husband to take the kids for a day. Even if you just take one day off, your time alone with the Lord will give you a fresh perspective. Your joy will be restored as you draw near to Him.

But here's the point—while you are in the state of needing refreshment, avoid the pattern of treating your husband badly. Don't be a grouch. Ask for help, yes. A kind word is much more likely to evoke a kind response.

Her children arise and call her blessed, her husband also, and he praises her.

Proverbs 31:28

7

A WIFE NEEDS HER HUSBAND'S

Praise and Support

Attributes of Praise and Support
- A husband should praise his wife for raising godly children
- A husband should praise his wife for maintaining their home
- A husband should praise his wife for her godliness and her beauty
- A husband should actively support his wife
- A husband should learn to speak his wife's love language

The virtuous woman described in Proverbs 31 works for a different set of rewards than the world offers these days. The world says get money, position, and power. A woman is told to seek her internal satisfaction from the externals the world has to offer. Many women who have chased after worldly success have realized that external rewards do not satisfy for very long.

One of the most important rewards, which has been proven by the test of time to really satisfy, is for a woman to receive genuine praise from her children and her husband. Studies on the differences between men and women show that men derive much of their sense of worth from their job. Women derive their sense of worth from their family. When a husband gives his wife genuine praise, he confirms that she is a worthy person who is accomplishing important goals.

Part of the reason that the feminists' ideology has been so successful is that the traditional accomplishments of wives and mothers have been taken for granted. Some men push their wives toward a feministic mindset when they make comments like, "That's what she's supposed to do. After all, she's a woman." An attitude like that will drive even the most traditionally minded woman into serious contemplation of the feminists' worldview. She will begin to think, "Maybe if I accomplish something different, something unexpected, maybe then I'll be respected and appreciated."

By choosing the lifestyle of Christian home schooling, you and your wife have made a joint decision that rejects the feminists' value system. This places a tremendous burden on you as the husband to make sure that your wife receives the appropriate praise for what she is doing and who she is. It is simply not fair to your wife to ask her to undertake so much responsibility and to do anything less than praise her from morning till night.

Praise Is Powerful

Words have power—power to build up and power to tear down. A sure-fire formula of building your wife up is to praise her often. If you want to make your wife feel worthless, only point out to her what she does wrong. Praising your wife is not complicated; you just need to tell her frequently what you appreciate about her. If you haven't given her much praise, she may respond skeptically at first: "What do you want?" If you have only poured on the praise to soften her up to get what you want, it may take her awhile to discern whether or not you are giving genuine praise.

People who struggle with a low self-concept will often discount praise. They will dismiss a compliment because they feel they don't deserve it. While Janine and I were at church one Sunday, she gave a woman a compliment. Janine said, "That is a pretty dress. I've never seen you wear it before. Is it new?"

The woman responded, "This dress. I did just get it. But it wasn't expensive. I paid five dollars for it at the mission store. In fact, I had to sew a button on it. So it's not really new. But this is the first time I've worn it."

She continued to point out flaws in the dress that no one would have ever noticed. By the time she was finished, I felt she had done everything she could to negate the compliment. She could not receive the praise she had been given because of her own low self-concept. Her husband's high degree of perfectionism probably contributed to her low self-esteem. Family members who live with a perfectionist often feel inadequate if they have been criticized often. If you are a perfectionist, you must work doubly hard to guard your tongue when you spot imperfection.

When Janine and I attended a weekend home school retreat, we spent some time talking with one couple whose marriage was obviously suffering as a result of the husband's critical spirit. In front of us, the husband openly criticized his wife's actions ("Why did you do that?"), her opinions ("That's silly!"), and her thoughts ("No one thinks like that!"). His belittling words were taking their toll. Her husband had beaten her down over time with his tongue. Her lack of confidence spilled over into every part of her life, including home schooling. Several times in our conversation she criticized herself. "I'm not a very good teacher...I could never teach that to my children." Her husband's words had power over her.

Do your words empower your wife or weaken her? Listen to yourself sometime. How often do you begin questions with *why*? *Why* questions tend to make people respond defensively. For example, "*Why* did you fold my shirts like that?" Or, "*Why* did you make that for dinner?" People naturally try to defend themselves when asked a *why* question. When people ask a *why* question, they usually don't care to hear the response. They just want to express their dissatisfaction.

Your wife has a built-in need for praise. How can you let your wife know that she is accomplishing important goals? Here are some suggestions:

1. Praise your wife for the important work she is doing with your children

Home schooling actually makes it easier for a husband to recognize the invaluable contributions his wife makes in the lives of their children. Home schooling has a perceived value that goes beyond just being a mom (which is extraordinarily important and highly under-recognized). But even though the home schooling mom deserves her husband's genuine praise, often her husband does not respond appropriately. Telling her once a year on Mother's Day that she's a great teacher is not enough. She needs to hear specific praise from her husband often.

Teaching kids at home is hard work, both physically and mentally. Unlike a traditional classroom teacher, your wife has to teach multiple subjects to multiple grade levels—quite a feat. Tell her how fantastic you think she is for pulling this off so successfully. Your wife needs all the encouragement she can get.

Praise her for modeling the Christian life to your children. A home schooling mom has the greatest opportunity of anyone in modern American life to model the Christian life in front of her children day after day, and year after year. At times she may not feel like she is having an impact on their spiritual lives, but you can encourage her by pointing out specific areas of growth that you have noticed in your children. Thank your wife for her obedience to Christ as she trains your children in the way they should go (Proverbs 22: 6).

Think of all the time and love your wife pours into the hearts of your little ones before they reach school age. A mother's love is the bedrock of your children's personality. She is the one who has built stability and security into the hearts of your children.

2. Praise her for the important work she does in maintaining your family home.

Keeping the house clean, the children fed, and the clothes washed is no easy task when you have a large family. Send your wife away on a weekend retreat and try to keep up the home like she does, and you will quickly realize how difficult her job is. You may want to greet her with flowers when she returns home.

Your wife needs to hear some positive reinforcement from you on two levels. First, she needs some straightforward appreciation for simply getting the job done. But on a deeper level, she needs to hear why her work is important to you and your family. She needs to hear specifics. Contemplate how your wife's dedication to the home contributes to the well-being of your family. How do her home-making efforts make a difference in the lives of your children? By her example, she is teaching your children how to manage their own household someday. Your children's children will be blessed by her efforts as your children follow her example.

Open your eyes and see all that your wife does for you, and then open your mouth with heavy-duty praise.

3. Praise her for her godliness

Neither you nor your wife will always be on a spiritual mountaintop. Every Christian walks through the desert at times, facing temptation to compromise what is right. You may come to a place where you are tempted to believe that walking with God is simply too hard. You may feel like taking a little vacation from the Christian life.

When I am down and tempted to think such thoughts, my wife has consistently pulled me back from the cliff and pushed me gently toward God. When I am spiritually weak, her spiritual vitality draws me back to the narrow path.

If your wife is a spiritual encourager in your life, praise her for her ministry to you.

4. Praise her for her beauty.

If you have any doubt about the appropriateness of praising your wife for her beauty, then you need to read the Song of Solomon again. I (Reed) try to lavish praise on my wife in this area because in her case it is very easy to do. In my humble opinion she is just plain gorgeous.

If you feel time has been unkind to your wife, just look at yourself in the mirror. How kind has time been to you? Nevertheless, no matter how old you are, beauty can always be discovered. Sometimes you just have to look harder for it. Remember, be specific in your praise. If you like her hair, tell her. If you like her clothing, make-up, eyes, physique, face, or smile, observe it and praise it.

Recognizing the beauty of your wife's appearance will work wonders for both of you. Praise will give your wife emotional reinforcement when she is tempted to worry about the cute twenty-eight-year-old who works in your office. Those words of genuine praise will be played back in the tape recorder of her mind when doubts and worries crop up. And you will be freshly reminded of how genuinely beautiful you find your wife to be when *you* see that cute twenty-eight-year-old.

The Three to One Rule

A study by marriage and family therapists found that for a relationship to keep a healthy equilibrium, three positive interactions were needed for every negative interaction. When there were three or more positive interactions, couples found it easier to handle the negative one.

Since most of us are not perfect, and we know that sooner or later we will mess up, we should deposit as many positive interactions into each other's love banks as possible. This will not erase or excuse negative behavior, but it may soften the blow. Sow mercy, and you will reap grace later.

Your Wife Needs Your Active Support

As a home school couple, both parents *are* working. One may work outside the home, usually the husband, and the wife works inside the home. Her work may include child-rearing, housekeeping, cooking, shopping, laundering, and more. Yet the home schooling mom adds another full-time job to her already long list of responsibilities. She is now a teacher. Dad assumes the role of teacher too, yet in most homes he does not teach as many subjects as mom does. The majority of the teaching responsibility is usually on mom's shoulders.

A husband can actively support his wife by being the kind of leader she needs.

Following Christ's Example

How does Christ lead the church? His leadership is gentle, loving, patient, and firm. He never badgers us or pushes us. When He was on earth, He spent His time ministering to the needs of people around Him and ultimately laid down his life for the world. He was a servant and an encourager, yet at the same time a man of authority.

When a husband leads like Christ does, his wife will naturally submit to him. He cannot force his wife to submit to him. Submission is an attitude of the heart. When a wife has trust and confidence that her husband will give his best for her and her family, she will follow willingly. Her allegiance and approval will also be there for him.

Many husbands desire authority but not responsibility. Authority and responsibility go hand in hand. Just as God has given men the authority over their homes, He has also given them full responsibility for their homes. That responsibility is not limited to bringing home a paycheck.

Just think of it this way: When a president of a company delegates a project to one of his vice presidents, he is ultimately responsible. When the president meets with his board of directors, he is asked if the project is finished. If the project is not finished, he can't blame his vice president. The board put him in charge. He is the one responsible. The buck stops with him.

As dad, the buck stops with you. You may delegate some tasks to your wife when you are gone, such as raising the children in the way you have agreed upon, disciplining as necessary, loving them, and teaching them; but when you return home, you must resume your role as head of the family. You cannot abdicate your God-given authority just because you don't want the responsibility. In the end you will stand before God and give an account to Him for how you handled the position you were given. You will have to answer to God someday.

Do the Dishes!

When I return home from work, I can tell exactly what kind of day it has been in my home by simply looking in the kitchen. On a good day the kitchen is clean; on a bad day there will be dishes stacked in the sink. Janine usually cleans up after a meal, but on one of those difficult home-schooling days sometimes the dishes rank lower on the priority list. I have learned that dirty dishes in the sink are no reflection on my wife's housekeeping skills, but that something more important needed her time. That something more important is usually one of our children.

As leader of the house, I have a choice. I can question my wife as to *why* the dishes are not washed and what she is going to do about it. Or, I can roll up my sleeves and get to work. I suggest the second option if you want to lead as Christ leads. Picture Jesus washing His disciples' smelly, dirty feet. Jesus—the master, the teacher, the leader—humbled Himself and served His followers, even one who would soon betray Him (John 13).

Jesus told the religious leaders of His day that He was their servant: "The greatest among you will be your servant. For whoever exalts himself will be humbled, and whoever humbles himself will be exalted" (Matthew 23:11,12). What a concept! Jesus turned the world upside down when He described leadership from God's perspective. He who has been given authority must become the greatest servant of all. Servant leaders do the dishes because they realize it is greater to serve than to be served.

As the head of my home I am responsible for everything in my home—that includes the dishes. So I do the dishes. Before I sound like some super spiritual giant, I must be honest. I don't like to do the dishes—especially when I was not there for the meal! But I do the dishes because of Jesus' example. To serve and support my wife, I take action rather than give rebuke when my wife is in need.

When husbands do not take responsibility, their wives are forced to take action. One home schooling wife who really desired some active support from her husband took matters into her own hands when he continued to ignore her needs. She asked her husband forty-eight times (twice a month for two years) if he could fix the freezer or move it out of the room so she could set up a laundry room in that particular room of their house. Finally, she got tired of asking and getting no action. Even though she was six months pregnant, she scooted, shoved, and pushed the freezer out the door into their backyard. The backyard was not where she desired the freezer to be, but her patience was a little thin after two years of waiting.

Communicate Support

A lot of men fail to communicate well because they learned poor habits from their fathers or they grew up in a dysfunctional family. To actively support your wife you must communicate with her. Your wife has no idea what is going on inside your head. Believe it or not, she is not clairvoyant after all.

Your wife needs your emotional support. Picture this scenario. You notice your wife is not herself lately. She seems tired, stressed, and short with the children occasionally. You say to yourself, "I know what she needs! I'll pick up a pizza on the way home from work and give her a break." You walk in the door feeling pretty good about yourself because you think you have fixed the problem. But her response is less than you hoped for. She thanks you, but your act of love seems to have made little difference in her mood. You may have misinterpreted her need. More than she needed a pizza, she needed a hug followed by encouraging words.

Fill Her Up!

Psychologists have identified love as a primary emotional need people have. History has shown us the lengths people will go to find and keep love. Antony and

Cleopatra were willing to go to war and ruin an empire for love. People fight, climb mountains, and perform extraordinary feats of courage, all for love. In the Bible, King Herod was willing to have John the Baptist beheaded because of love. Samson was willing to break tradition and God's laws, so he could marry a foreign girl.

God designed us with a deep need to be loved. Many counselors describe this need in terms of a tank that needs to be filled. This "love tank," as many counselors call it, is a holding tank, a reservoir for love. When our love tank is full we are content and happy with life. But when it is at a low level or empty, we do not feel loved. Bringing home a fast-food meal to your stressed wife may not be enough to fill up her tank. You may have correctly identified that your wife's love tank is running low, but your actions do not speak to her in a way that would fill up her tank. How do you fill up your wife's love tank? Learn her "love language."

Dr. Gary Chapman's book, *The Five Love Languages*[1] (which we highly recommend), explains that people have a unique "love language" that they desire most. The language that speaks to their heart fills up their tanks. People show their love and receive love from others differently. Dr. Chapman has pinpointed five ways people communicate love: with words, time, gifts, service, and physical touch.

1. Affirming words

A person who communicates love with words tells his wife he loves her often, and he needs to hear those words from her as well. He will compliment and encourage her when he wants to let her know he loves her. She fills his love tank when she tells him she loves him.

2. Quality time

A person who communicates love with his time will show his wife he loves her by doing something for her or with her. He feels loved when he and his wife have a quality conversation or do an activity together.

3. Thoughtful gifts

Another type of person shows love with gifts. He wants his wife to know that he is thinking of her and trying to meet her needs. He feels loved when his wife makes his favorite meal or surprises him with tickets to a game. The monetary value of the gift is not what counts, but the thoughtfulness of the gift.

4. Loving service

Communicating love through acts of service is another language of love. Doing the dishes for your wife or cleaning the garage are tasks that a husband may do to let his wife know he cares about her. When his wife cleans the house for him, her service shows him that she loves him.

5. Gentle touch

Some prefer to show love through touch. He lets his wife know he loves her every time he holds her hand, kisses her neck, gives her a backrub, or touches her hair. When his wife desires to have sex with him, she makes him feel loved. But sex is not the only form of touch that communicates love to him. When his wife puts her hand on his shoulder as she pours a drink at the table, rubs his shoulders while they stand at the kitchen sink, or sits close to him on the couch, he senses that she loves him.

One very critical point in Dr. Chapman's book is this: we each tend to use the "language" we want to hear when we are trying to express love to our spouse. I (Mike) have "affirming words" as my natural love language. I tend to give Vickie lots of verbal praise and love. Vickie has a tendency to speak "loving service" as her way of saying, "I love you." Vickie's challenge is to learn to give me more verbal praise. My challenge is to give her more acts of loving service.

People want to be loved in their own "native tongue." Spend some time talking with your spouse about your love languages. What communicates love to you? What makes your wife feel loved? Think back to when you first began your relationship. How did your spouse communicate love to you when you were dating? Did she encourage you often and tell you what a good job you were doing (words of affirmation)? Did she talk and listen to you for hours on the phone (quality time)? Did she give you little things, bake cookies for you, or write notes and put them on the windshield of your car (special gifts)? Did she do special jobs for you (acts of service)? Did she like to hold hands, walk arm in arm, and give you a hug when you needed one (gentle touch)? The language of love your spouse speaks is generally the language of love that fills up her love tank.

After you have talked and discovered your love language, make a plan of action. Make a list of things your spouse can do to fill up your love tank. Keep the list short, maybe five things she can do. Have her create a similar list for you. You can always add to the list later, but keep it simple at first. Exchange the lists and begin to work on blessing each other. Work at it for about one month. Then sit down and evaluate how it's going.

Husbands, you need to be the one to initiate followup. If you are meeting her desires on the list so far, you may both want to add to your lists some other ideas that would bless you and exchange lists again for another month. Lists force you to put your ideas into words. They also free your mind to think on other things instead of being bogged down with the task of remembering.

Learning to speak your spouse's love language may sound like a lot of work, but it will be worth the time and effort. It is one more way to meet the needs of your spouse effectively.

It's Worth It!

In my home it is my responsibility to make sure our vehicles are properly maintained. I (Reed) change the oil, check the fluid levels, change the wiper blades, wash the outside, vacuum the inside, and the list goes on. Why do I bother to do all of this? I was taught as I grew up that a properly maintained vehicle would last longer and should need fewer repairs than one that is neglected. My marriage is the same way. I can maintain it by blessing my spouse and meeting her needs so we have a smooth running relationship, or I can just drive it until something falls apart.

If you want to have a strong, affair-proof marriage, you must always remember: a good marriage takes work. The day you stop working at it is the day you stop having a good marriage. Take the time to meet your spouse's needs, and your relationship will grow and flourish throughout your married lives.

Notes

1. Dr. Gary Chapman, *The Five Love Languages* (Chicago, IL: Northfield Press, 1992).

The Secret to a Great Marriage

*W*hat is the secret to a great marriage? The secret is a simple concept yet impossible to do in your own strength. Jesus asks you to "lay down your life" (John 15:13) and become a servant. When we give up, He takes over. The secret is told in these verses:

> Greater love has no one than this, that he lay down his life for his friends. (John 15:13)

> I have been crucified with Christ and I no longer live, but Christ lives in me. The life I live in the body, I live by faith in the Son of God, who loved me and gave Himself for me. (Galatians 2:20)

181

> Whoever wants to become great among you must be your servant, and whoever wants to be first must be slave of all. For even the Son of Man did not come to be served, but to serve, and to give His life as a ransom for many. (Mark 10:43-45)

The recurring theme is this: die to self and serve others. Give up trying to meet your needs and start trying to meet your spouse's needs. Look at Jesus' example. He had full authority over heaven and earth, yet He lived to serve and died to give us eternal life. He was not a dictator or an authoritarian leader. As He healed the sick, fed the masses, and supped with the sinners, He modeled how to be a servant leader. He filled his "love tank" with the Father's love and continued to pour out His love on others.

Your spouse will disappoint you over and over again. He or she is bound to fail at times. Instead of looking to your spouse to make you feel better, look to God to make you feel better. Jesus tells you to "remain in My love" (John 15:9). When you remain in His love, His joy will be in you and your joy will be complete (John 15:11). He will make you a fountain welling up with water, rather than a dry hole. When you look up (at Christ), you will get your needs met. When you look sideways (at your wife) to get your needs met, you will find disappointment. In looking up, you become a blessing rather than a burden. The first person to be blessed is you as you experience the presence of the living God in your inner being. This is a transforming experience and gives you the ability that is beyond your human limits to meet the needs of others and to point them by example to the Great I Am.

Marriage is not about giving fifty-fifty. That is man's way of thinking. Marriage requires giving 100 percent of yourself at all times even when you receive nothing in return. It is not a give-and-take relationship. It is a give-and-give relationship.

Have the Christlike attitude, "How can I bless you?" Focus on how you can be a blessing to your spouse rather than how your spouse should be a blessing to you. If both of you have the same giving attitude, you will both be blessed. But don't wait for your spouse to bless you. When you focus on getting your own needs met through your spouse instead of from God, you will always come up short.

You may be thinking, "Yeah, but what about when he acts like a selfish jerk? He doesn't deserve to be blessed." When your spouse is undeserving of kindness, then focus on your accountability to God. You are individually accountable to God for what you do, don't do, say, and think. You may feel like your spouse doesn't deserve mercy, but Christ does. Christ wants you to love even when it's tough.

> But love your enemies, do good to them, and lend to them without expecting to get anything back. Then your reward will be great, and you will be sons of the Most High, because He is kind to the ungrateful and wicked. (Luke 6:35)

Walking in Christ's shoes means giving away your shoes at times. The path may hurt your feet, but Christ will be right there beside you as you give yourself away. You cannot do it without holding His hand. You will burnout eventually. You must continuously draw your strength from Him. Remember Christ's words:

> I am the vine; you are the branches. If a man remains in Me and I in him, he will bear much fruit; apart from Me you can do nothing. (John 15:5)

When you serve, keep in mind whose servant you are. Remember Colossians 4:23-25: "Whatever you do, work at it with all your heart, as working for the Lord, not for men, since you know that you will receive an inheritance from the Lord as a reward. It is the Lord Christ you are serving."

Love as Christ would have you love your spouse, and your relationship will be transformed. Ask Christ to change you in the areas that hinder you from blessing your husband or wife. Maybe you need strength to lead or to submit, to show compassion or allegiance, to give praise and encouragement. Whatever area you are weak in, ask Christ to show you how to improve. Recognizing the need to change is the first step. Submitting to Christ to change you is the second. If you are humble and willing to accept His leadership in your life, He will change you. He is just waiting for you to ask.